Bloom's
GUIDES

Margaret Atwood's
The Handmaid's Tale

D0169060

1984
All the Pretty Horses
Beloved
Brave New World
Cry, The Beloved Country
Death of a Salesman
Hamlet
The Handmaid's Tale
The House on Mango Street
I Know Why the Caged Bird Sings
The Scarlet Letter
To Kill a Mockingbird

Bloom's
GUIDES

Margaret Atwood's
The Handmaid's Tale

Edited & with an Introduction
by Harold Bloom

CHELSEA HOUSE
PUBLISHERS
A Haights Cross Communications Company
Philadelphia

Introduction © 2004 by Harold Bloom.

Printed and bound in the United States of America.

First Printing
1 3 5 7 9 8 6 4 2

Library of Congress Cataloging-in-Publication Data
Applied.
ISBN: 0-7910-7569-9

Chelsea House Publishers
1974 Sproul Road, Suite 400
Broomall, PA 19008-0914

www.chelseahouse.com

Contributing editor: Jenn McKee and Frank Diamond

Cover series and design by Takeshi Takahashi

Layout by EJB Publishing Services

Contents

Introduction

Harold Bloom

Literary survival, as such, was not my overt subject when I started out as a critic, over a half-century ago, but I have aged into an exegete who rarely moves far from a concern with the question: Will it last? I have little regard for the ideologies— feminist, Marxist, historicist, deconstructive—that tend to dominate both literary study and literary journalism. Margaret Atwood seems to me vastly superior as a critic of Atwood to the ideologues she attracts. My brief comments upon *The Handmaid's Tale* will be indebted to Atwood's own published observations, and if I take any issue with her, it is with diffidence, as she herself is an authentic authority upon literary survival.

I first read *The Handmaid's Tale* when it was published, in 1986. Rereading it remains a frightening experience, even if one lives in New Haven and New York City, and not in Cambridge, Massachusetts, where the Handmaid Offred suffers the humiliations and torments afflicted upon much of womankind in the Fascist Republic of Gilead, which has taken over the Northeastern United States. Atwood, in describing her novel as a dystopia, called it a cognate of *A Clockwork Orange*, *Brave New World*, and *Nineteen Eighty-Four*. All of these, are now period pieces. Anthony Burgess's *A Clockwork Orange*, despite its Joycean wordplay, is a much weaker book than his memorable *Inside Enderby*, or his superb *Nothing Like the Sun*, persuasively spoken by Shakespeare-as-narrator. Aldous Huxley's *Brave New World* now seems genial but thin to the point of transparency, while George Orwell's *Nineteen Eighty-Four* is just a rather bad fiction. These prophecies do not caution us. London's thugs, like New York City's, are not an enormous menace; Henry Ford does not seem to be the God of the American Religion; Big Brother is not yet watching us, in our realm of virtual reality. But theocracy is a live menace: in Iran and the recently deposed Taliban, in the influence of the Christian Coalition upon the Republican Party, and on a much smaller scale, in the tyranny over English-speaking universities of our New Puritans, the academic feminists. *The Handmaid's Tale*, even if it did not have authentic aesthetic value (and it does), is not at all a period piece under our current circumstances. The Right-to-Life demagogues rant on, urging that the Constitution be amended, and while contemporary Mormonism maintains its repudiation of plural marriage, the Old Faith of Joseph Smith and Brigham Young is practiced by polygamists in Utah and adjacent states.

Atwood says of *The Handmaid's Tale*: "It is an imagined account of what happens when not uncommon pronouncements about women are taken to their logical conclusions." Unless there is a Swiftian irony in that sentence, which I cannot quite hear, I am moved to murmur: just when and where, in the world of Atwood and her readers, are those not uncommon pronouncements being made? There are a certain number of Southern Republican senators, and there is the leadership of the Southern Baptist convention, and some other clerical Fascists, who perhaps would dare to make such pronouncements, but "pronouncements" presumably have to be public, and you don't get very far by saying that a woman's place is in the home. Doubtless we still have millions of men (and some women) who in private endorse the Bismarckian formula for women: *Kinder, Kirche, und Kuchen*, but they do not proclaim these sentiments to the voters.

Atwood makes a less disputable point when she warns us about the history of American Puritanism, which is long and dangerous. Its tendencies are always with us, and speculative fictions from Hawthorne to Atwood legitimately play upon its darkest aspects. *The Handmaid's Tale* emerges from the strongest strain in Atwood's imaginative sensibility, which is Gothic. A Gothic dystopia is an oddly mixed genre, but Atwood makes it work. Offred's tone is consistent, cautious, and finally quite frightening. Atwood, in much, if not most, of her best poetry and prose, writes Northern Gothic in the tradition of the Brontës and of Mary Shelley. Though acclaimed by so many Post-Modernist ideologues, Atwood is a kind of late Victorian novelist, and all the better for it. Her Gilead, at bottom, is a vampiric realm, a society sick with blood. *The Handmaid's Tale* is a brilliant Gothic achievement, and a salutary warning to keep our Puritanism mostly in the past.

Biographical Sketch

Margaret Eleanor Atwood was born on November 18, 1939 in Ottawa, Ontario, the second child of Carl Edmund Atwood and Margaret Killam Atwood. Her brother, Harold, was born in 1937 and her sister Ruth in 1951. Soon after Atwood's birth the family moved to rural northwestern Quebec, where they would spend several months of each year as her father pursued studies in forest entomology. In 1946, the family began alternating spring, summer, and fall in the Canadian wilderness with winters in Toronto, where Carl Atwood joined the University of Toronto faculty.

Atwood learned to read at a young age and was particularly fond of Grimms' *Fairy Tales*, whose influence, along with the wilderness survival themes of her childhood, are evident in her later writing. She began writing plays, poems, stories and comics at age six, but did not consider professional writing until sixteen, when she determined to become a poet. After graduating from Leaside High School in Toronto in 1957, Atwood enrolled at Victoria College, University of Toronto where she studied English Literature in order to teach to support her poetry. In 1959, "Fruition" was published in a major literary journal, *The Canadian Forum*, which gave her an "in" to the tight-knit Canadian poetry scene of P. K. Page, Jay MacPherson (one of her professors), Leonard Cohen, and A. M. Klein, among others. In 1961 she graduated from University of Toronto and published *Double Persephone*, which was awarded the prestigious E.J. Pratt Medal for Poetry.

Atwood moved to Boston where she received a Master's in English from Radcliffe College in 1962. She continued her studies for a graduate degree at Harvard, and though they were incomplete she was awarded several honorary degrees between 1973 and 1990, from Trent University, Queen's University, Concordia University, Radcliffe, and Harvard. In 1964 she taught creative writing at the University of British Columbia, the first of several teaching/writer-in-residence appointments at reputable North American universities, including University of Alberta (1968–70), University of Toronto (1971–73), New York University (1971–72), and University of British Columbia (1964–65, 1992–93).

In 1967, the collection *The Circle Game* (1966) won the Governor-General's Award for Poetry, securing her reputation as a poet. In 1967, she married James Polk, and in 1969 her first work of fiction, *The Edible Woman*, was published, followed by *The Journals of Susanna Moodie* (1970) and *Surfacing* (1971). After traveling in England, France and Italy from 1970–71, Atwood began a two year stint as Editor and member of the board of directors at the influential Canadian publishing House of Anansi Press. She published a seminal work in Canadian literary criticism in 1972, *Survival: A Thematic Guide to Canadian Literature*.

In 1973 Atwood and Polk divorced, and she wrote the first of several screenplays, *Grace Marks*, whose protagonist would become the central character in her 1996 novel, *Alias Grace*. In 1973, she and author Graeme Gibson began living together, and in 1976 their daughter Eleanor Jess Atwood Gibson was born. Atwood continued to publish at a prolific rate: *Lady Oracle* (1976), *Two-Headed Poems* (1978), *Life Before Man* (1979), and several works for children rounded out the decade.

In 1980, Atwood served as Co-chair of the Writer's Union of Canada. In the same year she received a Guggenhiem Fellowship and the Molson Award, and published *Bodily Harm*. In 1983 she received the foundation for the Advancement of Canadian Letters Book of the Year Award for the short story collection *Bluebeard's Egg*, and served as President of International P.E.N., Canadian Centre from 1984–86. In 1985 one of her most influential works of fiction, *The Handmaid's Tale*, was published to critical acclaim. It continues to be one of the most widely taught novels in North American colleges. In 1988, *Cat's Eye* was published, followed by *Wilderness Tips* in 1991 and *Good Bones* in 1992. In 1992 after nearly a decade of travel—to Germany and England with teaching positions held in Australia, New York, Alabama, and Texas—Atwood returned to Toronto, where she continues to live with Graeme Gibson. The last decade has seen the publication of *The Robber Bride*

11

(1993), *Good Bones and Simple Murders* (1994), *Strange Things: The Malevolent North in Canadian Literature* (1995), *Mornings in the Burned House* (1995), *Alias Grace* (1996), and *Negotiating With the Dead: A Writer on Writing* (2002). Her novel *The Blind Assassin* was awarded The Booker Prize in 2000, the most prestigious honor in British letters.

The Story Behind the Story

Susan Faludi once noted that feminists were "a prime enemy" for the New Right that evolved in America during the 1980's, and to understand this point *fully* is to understand *The Handmaid's Tale*'s true point of origin. In *Brutal Choreographies*, for example, critic J. Brooks Bouson noted that at this time, Jerry Falwell accused feminists of executing "a satanic attack on the home," and, similarly, Howard Phillips argued that feminists schemed for "the conscious policy of government to liberate the wife from the leadership of the husband" (135). In this way, through every form of media, women were being told daily to get back into the kitchen; if they refused, they reportedly did so at the expense of children and families—and thus, by extension, America's future.

But one night in 1981, shortly after the publication of *Bodily Harm*, Margaret Atwood had dinner with a long-time friend, unaware that this casual get-together would spark the idea for *The Handmaid's Tale*. According to Atwood's own report, the two women discussed "various things as we usually do, including some of the more absolutist pronouncements of right-wing religious fundamentalism. 'No one thinks about what it would be like to actually act it out,' said I (or someone)". Atwood took this very task upon herself.

The seeds for a novel thus took root, though Atwood didn't pursue the project in earnest until, ironically, 1984. The resonance of that year—the title and subject of George Orwell's own classic, cautionary tale—seems no mere coincidence. Before writing *Handmaid*, Atwood read and studied numerous utopian and dystopian works: not only Orwell's, but also Thomas More's (*Utopia*) and Aldous Huxley's (*Brave New World*), among others. She also continued to read the Bible closely, drawing inspiration from Genesis 30, and she kept a running file of newspaper and magazine clippings about contemporary world crises. According to critic Coral Ann Howells, the file included:

pamphlets from Friends of the Earth and Greenpeace ... beside reports of atrocities in Latin America, Iran and the Philippines, together with items of information on new reproductive technologies, surrogate motherhood, and forms of institutionalized birth control from Nazi Germany to Ceausescu's Romania.... The clippings file contain[ed] a lot of material on the New Right with its warnings about the "Birth Dearth," its anti-feminism, its anti-homosexuality, its racism and its strong underpinnings in the Bible Belt.

The materials Atwood collected thus show the breadth of her concerns on a large scale, but they also pinpoint her particular obsessions: the environment, intolerance, fascism, and reproductive rights. And because she takes pains to mention what were, at the time, current events within the world of the novel, she clearly strives to present "a fictive future which bears an uncomfortable resemblance to our present society"

Critics often note, of course, that Atwood, a Canadian writer, makes the choice to set Gilead within America's boundaries. Rather than simply wagging a finger, however, in an act of reductive, literary censure, Atwood provides cogent reasons for her setting choice in interviews. For example, she once stated of the novel's premise:

It's not a Canadian sort of thing to do. Canadians might do it after the States did it, in some sort of watered-down version. Our television evangelists are more paltry than yours. The States are more extreme in everything.

Our genius is for compromise... That's number one. And I lived in Boston/Cambridge for four years. That's number two. And then they are my ancestors. Those nagging Puritans really are my ancestors. So I had a considerable interest in them when I was studying them, and the mind-set of Gilead is really close to that of the seventeenth-century Puritans. It's also true that everyone watches the States to see what the country is doing and might be doing ten or fifteen years from now.

Thus, the influence of the Puritans—which still resonates in American cultural norms—and the bold, arrogant, spotlight-hogging image that still typifies the United States, made it the ideal setting for Atwood to ponder questions like, "If a woman's place is in the home, what happens when women want more? If means are taken to enforce a stay-at-home regime, what follows?"

Obviously, the answers Atwood offers in *The Handmaid's Tale* have successfully captured readers' imaginations; with the exception of a handful of reviews, the book generally received positive critical response, and, as Sharon R. Wilson reported, the novel has become the most widely-taught Atwood text in the country. At the college level, the book shows up on the syllabi of courses in "economics, political science, sociology, film, business, and other disciplines outside the humanities, and it has been adopted by several universities (e.g., George Mason, Miami University) as a required text for all undergraduates". Thus, though some critics have pointed out the work's flaws, the continuing relevance of the novel's themes and Atwood's distinctive exploration of them have caused *The Handmaid's Tale* to become a part of the contemporary literature canon.

List of Characters

Offred, the novel's narrator—and the Handmaid whose "tale" is re-constructed—had been a working wife and mother before the Republic of Gilead evolved. Captured while trying to escape to Canada with her husband and daughter, she is trained as a Handmaid: that is, a woman who will act solely as a reproductive mechanism in the home of a highly-placed figure in the new government. Her given name, which remains a mystery, is replaced with the patronymic "**Offred,**" marking her as a possession of a Gileadean Commander ("of Fred"). The name's other association, however—"off-red"—hints that she is not as devout as she first appears.

Offred acts on her impulses toward revolt, but with definite restraint. Atwood states of her creation, "The voice is that of an ordinary, more-or-less cowardly woman (rather than heroine), because I suppose I'm more interested in social history than in the biographies of the outstanding." Offred's decision to forego involvement in the clandestine resistance movement for the smaller freedoms of an affair with the chauffeur, Nick, and the opportunity to read and speak again in evening meetings with the Commander, has led some critics to surmise she is complicit in her own imprisonment.

Offred tells her story through first person narration; because she isn't allowed to write, readers believe, throughout the course of the book, that they simply have access to the Handmaid's thoughts. However, at the conclusion, readers discover that the "tale" was recovered from a series of audio cassette tapes in Maine, indicating she likely escaped the regime. Though the tale is compelling, Offred reminds readers throughout the narrative that her subjective lens is altering and guiding the tale as she tells it—making her somewhat unreliable as a narrator—but also, readers learn at the end, male historians edited, ordered, and transcribed her story.

The "banality of evil" is the phrase one associates with the **Commander**, suspected by historians (who appear in the novel's final section) to be Fred Waterford, a high ranking, key player in the regime. He designed the Handmaids' red habits and proposed plans for executing punishment rituals (among other things), but to Offred, he appears as a gray-haired, impotent, fatherly figure, pitiable in his emotional distance from his wife, Serena Joy, and pathetic in his need for Offred's sympathy and understanding. Though it goes against the laws he helped create, he sets up regular one-on-one meetings with Offred a few evenings a week, wherein they play Scrabble and talk. Oftentimes, he gives her small gifts, like lotion or an old magazine, treating her like a child. On one occasion, he makes her dress in a gaudy, sleazy outfit (with feathers and sequins) to take her to the underground "club" Jezebel's, a hotel where he propositions Offred, complaining that the institutionalized sex of the monthly, state-sanctioned Ceremony—which involves Offred staying dressed and leaning her head back on the Wife's belly while the Commander works to impregnate her—is "impersonal."

Ultimately, the Commander has become disillusioned with the world he helped to create and hungers now for the type of woman he marginalized; he still looks to Offred, for example, for validation, wanting his indulgences to her to be repaid with respect and affection, and asking her in earnest, "What did we overlook?" He can't see the fissures and injustices of his system, in spite of his own compunction to commit acts against it, because he is the one with power. And sadly, based on the tone of the historians' discussion at the novel's conclusion, we see that in some ways, he remains in power; for in pursuit of authenticating the audio tapes, the historians concentrate on recovering the identity of the Commander, thus defining Offred yet again in relation to her jailer.

For **Serena Joy (the Commander's Wife)**, the wife of the Commander, Offred is a constant reminder of lost youth and vitality, as well as a symbol of the Commander's state-sanctioned adultery, which humiliates her. She shows obvious disdain for Offred, ignoring her whenever possible, and trying by every means to shorten the monthly "Ceremony" in which the Commander copulates with Offred. In spite of her behavior, however, Serena Joy wants a baby—*the* status symbol in Gileadean society—so she arranges for Offred to meet with Nick, the chauffeur, in the dark of night. When she approaches Offred with this idea, the full measure of her cruelty is exposed: she offers to let Offred see a current photo of her daughter if she agrees to meet with him. Yet Serena Joy reveals a kind of vulnerability: when she finds the revealing outfit that Offred wore to the club with the Commander, Serena Joy unleashes her feelings of betrayal. Offred realizes that Serena still genuinely cares for the Commander, despite their apparent emotional distance.

Serena Joy appears to be a composite of anti-feminist women who were in the news at the time Atwood wrote *The Handmaid's Tale*: specifically, Tammy Faye Baker, the perpetually weeping, earnest, mascara-stained wife of televangelist Jim Baker (jailed for defrauding the public and publicly embarrassed by an affair with his former secretary); and Phyllis Schlafly, an icon of the American conservative movement who spearheaded the drive to defeat the Equal Rights Amendment. Serena Joy, who Offred recalls having the real name of "Pam," had been a singer on a gospel show pre-Gilead, and she eventually became a vocal proponent of women's re-installation in the home; as Offred notes, however, her activism and speechmaking meant that she did not practice what she preached, and this leads Offred, after seeing Serena Joy languish in her garden or knit in her sitting room, bored and smoking, to remark, "How furious she must be, now that she's been taken at her word."

Nick, the Commander's chauffeur, startles Offred with his casual attitudes and his blatant disregard for the strict rules of the regime. Readers first see him when he speaks casually to Offred and winks at her; later, he kisses her, at once re-awakening her feelings of tenderness, lust, and hope. Nick is bold in his disregard for the new customs, but his larger function in the novel is that of a potential replacement for Luke (Offred's husband). Nick acts as the go-between for the

Commander and Offred's secret meetings, and also for Serena Joy, who arranges to have Offred sleep with Nick in an attempt to get her pregnant. An affair grows from this encounter, to the point that Offred feels herself falling in love with Nick; she recklessly goes to his apartment many nights; she smiles to herself around the house; and she begins to feel content in the life she has established for herself. But Offred struggles with the guilt that comes with her feelings for Nick, afraid that she is betraying Luke. Near the end of the novel he arranges for Offred's escape, perhaps to his own detriment, in order to save her and, as the historians speculate, the child she might be carrying.

Moira is Offred's best friend from college, her confidant, and her hero, unafraid of the consequences of speaking and acting against Gilead. As critic Glenn Deer notes, "Atwood is continually tempted to endow Offred with the strength appropriate to a heroine, but instead she assigns the spectacular heroism to Moira, who mounts a daring escape from the Red Center, an act of such dizzying audacity that it frightens Offred and the others who 'were losing the taste for freedom.'" Indeed, Moira's second attempt at escape succeeds, leaving Offred wondering, for much of the novel, what's become of her friend, but hoping that her brazen attempt for freedom was a success (and thus, that her own may be possible). Offred is disappointed, though, when she sees Moira as one of the regular party girls at the Commander's club. Instead of the lesbian feminist activist by which Offred had measured her life, she finds a woman resigned to her fate, happy for the chance to be with other women at the club. The fall of Offred's hero disturbs the narrator, such that she feels that if her strong friend can be broken, made content with small bits of happiness, than there is no hope for any of them.

If Moira is a benchmark for outspokenness, then **Janine** stands as the supreme example of what can happen when one buys into Gilead's regime. An accomplice to her own enslavement as a Handmaid, she admits that her rape and subsequent abortion at age 14 were her fault; this puts her in the good graces of the Aunts. Later, as Ofwarren, Janine becomes pregnant by secretly allowing the doctor to impregnate her during a monthly visit. Janine wears her pregnancy like a badge, but after the baby is born and placed in the arms of Warren's wife, it soon dies, and Janine is transferred to another commander. Reader's last see Janine at the Particicution, a ceremony in which Handmaids may do whatever they wish to a man who has, they're told, committed rape and murdered a baby. She is seen carrying a tuft of the man's hair, smiling, and Offred notes that "her eyes have become loose"—after years of bowing to the regime, she is becoming unhinged, and serves as a kind of warning to Offred. She also exists as a polar opposite to Moira, providing Offred with two extreme examples to watch from her place in the crowded middle ground.

Ofglen is a fellow Handmaid and Offred's shopping partner. At first, Ofglen seems pious, a "true believer" who prays and goes to the Wall out of duty, and Offred realizes that she must appear the same way to Ofglen. Ofglen begins to reveal her true identity as a resistance member when she asks Offred, in front of the Soul Scrolls window, "Do you think God listens to these machines?" Offred recognizes that even the question is sacrilegious, so she responds, "No," and they then begin to speak with each other in a more casual, more conspiratorial way. Ofglen tells Offred about the "Mayday" code word, which identifies resisters, and encourages her to participate in the spying game, urging her to find out as much as she can during her evening visits with the Commander. But it is too much of a risk for Offred, who declines involvement. Ofglen's own dedication to the cause is most fully demonstrated at the Salvaging, where she is the first to attack the "suspect," kicking him to death. When Offred castigates her, Ofglen explains that he was "one of ours" and that she had put him out of his misery; after the ceremony, Ofglen sees a black van coming for her and hangs herself, and Offred, frightened that Ofglen would tell the authorities about her, sees this as Ofglen dying so that she may live. Though perhaps not as bold as Moira,

Ofglen still presents to Offred another choice about how to live in her circumstances, working in small ways to overthrow the system.

Luke, Offred's husband, makes his appearance only in flashbacks when she thinks about her life before the revolution. Throughout the narrative, Offred maintains hope that he escaped during their attempt to cross the border with their five-year-old daughter. Luke and Offred were married after an extra-marital affair and his divorce; this is the reason Offred is cast as Handmaid in Gilead's strict regime. The chauffeur Nick acts as a foil to him, giving Offred the opportunity to love once more after three years apart from her husband, a fact which makes her feel guilty.

Offred's Daughter, like her mother, remains nameless throughout the novel; readers only catch short glimpses of her through flashbacks; during Offred and Luke's attempted escape to Canada, for instance, when mother and daughter were captured and separated. Three years later, Offred sees her daughter once in a photograph; at eight years old, she wears a long, white dress, similar to those the daughters wear at the Prayvaganza, where arranged marriages to soldiers take place. Offred senses that this will be her daughter's fate, and mourns the fact that she has most likely been erased from her daughter's mind. She continues to hope they will one day be reunited, but the book does not tell us whether she sees her husband or daughter again.

Offred's Mother, who also only appears in flashbacks, was in pre-Gilead a pioneer of the radical wing of the women's movement, a "pronatalist" who decided to have Offred at age thirty-seven and raise her without the aid of a male counterpart. She takes part in marches and pornography bonfires, and although she claims to fight for women's equality, Atwood seems to make her, by her actions, a proponent of women's supremacy. Thus, although Offred's mother (significantly also never named) is another strong female character, she also represents yet another extreme. At one point, Moira tells Offred that she spotted her mother while watching a film about women working in the Colonies, cleaning up toxic dumps and radiation spills. Even though the "women's society" she wanted has, in a perverse way, been achieved, she has been marginalized more severely than ever before.

Cora and Rita (The Marthas) are, in the Commander's household, Marthas: older women beyond the child-rearing age who work as domestic servants. The two women make for a sort of a good/bad cop combination; Cora sees Offred's reproductive capabilities as hope and potential happiness, and acts with small courtesies toward Offred, knocking on her door and smiling and slipping her cookies as though she is indulging a child.

Rita, on the other hand, hates and harshly judges Offred for choosing the life of a Handmaid over banishment to the Colonies. However, she comes to treat Offred with a bit more deference when she sees that Serena Joy has extended more privileges to her (rewards for her agreeing to meet with Nick). The Marthas offer a perspective on how post-menopausal women in the system regard the new order, centered around, and obsessed with, fertility. The Marthas' gossip and their comments on society, which Offred often overhears, are informal and candid, and she longs to be a part of the community they've established among themselves.

Aunt Lydia and Aunt Elizabeth are the two main wardens of the Red Center, whose job is to indoctrinate the new Handmaids for their roles in the Republic of Gilead. When seen through flashbacks, they often serve the purpose of reminding Offred how to act in different circumstances. They constantly spout platitudes and slogans against immodesty, reading and writing, and materialism, and they champion women's traditional maternal role, encouraging the Handmaids to think of the new system as a means of forming a meaningful, positive community of women. As one of the bulwarks of the

Republic of Gilead, the Aunts' positions were created (perhaps with the Commander's help, we learn) based on the supposition that the best way to control women is through other women. Offred is surrounded by women who have made choices about their place in a new society, and the Aunts represent one of the lowest group: those willing to harm and sacrifice others for the sake of their own self-interest.

Summary and Analysis

Margaret Atwood's controversial, feminist dystopian novel, *The Handmaid's Tale* (1984), features the ruminations of a female prisoner in Gilead—a theocratic dictatorship that evolves, in the near future, within America's borders. This oppressive regime measures a woman's worth solely by her reproductive capabilities (adhering to a "biology as destiny" philosophy), and women are not allowed to read, write, hold property, or have a job. In this way, Atwood deliberately magnifies and exaggerates the tradition-based ideology of America's religious right, or moral majority of the early 1980s, so as to scrutinize possible social consequences.

The novel is told through the eyes of Offred, a Handmaid whose function in the new regime is to bear children for a couple in the largely barren ruling class. Importantly, the novel is told by recollection—sequences of remembered events in which daily happenings are separated by sections of "night." As an unwilling (though as critics have noted, complicit) participant of Gilead, Offred struggles with the question, "If this is to be my life, is it better to remember or forget?" Apparently she chooses to remember, for in the final section of the book, we find the story was in fact recorded on a series of audiotapes found in a "safe house" after the Gileadean regime's demise, and their dictation serves as a key document at a conference of "Gileadean studies." Readers must additionally consider that while Offred struggles to construct herself through language, her internal, raging battle between self-preservation and human dignity manifests itself in this jagged presentation, and re-creation, of her identity.

I Night

The novel begins in the time of Offred's indoctrination. She and other Handmaids-in-training wait in an area that had once been a school gymnasium (now the Rachel and Leah Re-education Center). In this brief but dense scene, Offred attempts to construct her reality fact by fact, recording precise details about her surroundings, but also remembering their original functions—basketball games and school dances, which remind her of the hopeful period of adolescence. In sharp contrast to her past sense of wonder, Offred explains how the women in the gym are lying in rows of cots, with spaces in between so they can't speak to each other, and how the "Aunts," armed with cattle prods, patrol the area. Male guards, or "Angels," patrol the area but aren't allowed inside the complex, remind Offred of the sexual tension apparent when rules are enforced.

Offred also explains how, in the dark of the night, the women reach across the space between their beds and mouth their names to each other, demonstrating from the outset that Gilead's indoctrination will fail to penetrate beyond the surface. Ironically, of course, these women's deprivation provides them all with a kind of adolescent innocence again; they hope for the thrill of a forbidden male's glance, and the simple touch of hands becomes charged with a sense of revolt and power.

II Shopping

In **Chapter 2,** Offred continues to record the details of her surroundings: now a room in the Commander's house where she serves as Handmaid. Noting the lack of anything that may serve as a means for suicide—no chandelier, no breakable glass—Atwood emphasizes her constant but subtle vigilance for means of escape.

Offred next likens her world to a nunnery, where there are few mirrors, and time is measured in ringing bells. She pulls on shoes, gloves, and a body-hiding dress that are "the color of blood," calling up not only images of menstruation (and thus reproduction), but also Hester Prynne's scarlet "A." Only the wimple, which hides Offred's face and prevents her from seeing others', is white. "I never looked good in red, it's not my color," Offred says, revealing her sense of dissociation, as does her name; its origins lie in the conjunction of the words "of Fred," the Commander, but the conjoined word's other interpretation indicates that the narrator is not truly, in mind and spirit, a true believer. She is "off-red." (Critics note also the name's similarity to "offered" and "afraid.")

After dressing, Offred picks up a basket to go shopping, suggesting an image of a grown-up Red Riding Hood ("some fairy tale figure in a red cloak, descending towards a moment of carelessness that is the same as danger")—not surprising, since Atwood's work very often alludes to folk and fairy tales. Indeed, Offred even describes the hallway outside her room as resembling "a path through the forest." And eventually shopping, though strictly regimented, does provide Offred with an opportunity to stray slightly from the figurative path (that is, the rules), and this small taste of rebellion eventually puts her in danger.

When Offred leaves her room, she goes to the kitchen, where Rita and Cora, clad in green, work as Marthas. Offred admits that she listens to them talk sometimes, including a conversation wherein Rita argues that Handmaids don't have to debase themselves—that they have the choice to become Unwomen and go to the Colonies to take their chances cleaning toxic dumps. Cora argues, however, that this isn't a choice at all. This conversation demonstrates not only the propensity for gossip among women, but also the capacity they have for turning on, and judging, each other, particularly in times of crisis. Despite Rita's harsh judgment, however, Offred confesses that she longs to talk to the Marthas the way they do to each other, realizing how much comfort this sense of community would afford her. But she notes that such fraternization is outlawed, a thought that leads to her first reminiscence of her pre-Gilead husband Luke, who, significantly, had spoken to her about the lack of a female version of the word "fraternize." Offred accepts food tokens from the Marthas and leaves.

In **Chapter 3**, Offred walks through the garden, "the domain of the Commander's Wife," and remembers that she once had a garden herself. She tells us that the Wife often works and sits in the garden or knits childish scarves for the Angels at the front lines (this is the first hint of an ongoing war).

Offred next recalls the first time she and the Commander's Wife met, five weeks before.

The Wife had blocked the doorway, dismissed the Guardian who accompanied Offred, and then finally led her to the sitting room. There, the Wife had smoked cigarettes, which indicated that she had access to the black market—an observation that filled Offred with hope: "there's always something that can be exchanged." Meanwhile, the Wife asked about Offred's previous post and learns that this was her third—a significant milestone, for if Handmaids fail to conceive after three postings, they are sent off to starve and work in the dreaded Colonies as Unwomen.

"I want to see as little of you as possible.... I expect you feel the same way about me," the Wife tells Offred, who doesn't answer. "As far as I'm concerned, this is like a business transaction," she continued. Offred agrees but secretly yearns for a mother figure, "someone who would understand and protect" her. And though she knows that she will not have this relationship with the Wife, Offred wonders why the Wife looks familiar. Soon, she recognizes her as Serena Joy, the lead soprano on a gospel television show that had aired before the revolution.

In **Chapter 4**, Offred walks toward the house's front gate and passes, in the driveway, a Guardian who's washing the Commander's car. Like the Wife, Nick smokes a black market cigarette, and as Offred walks by, he winks at her. Offred drops her head, feeling confused and scared; Nick may be an Eye, she thinks, a spy of the new regime.

At the street corner, Offred waits for her shopping partner, Ofglen, to arrive, since Handmaids may only travel in pairs. When Ofglen appears, the two women recite biblical, government-sanctioned greetings ("Blessed be the fruit" and "May the Lord Open") and head toward town. Offred notes that the current incarnation of Ofglen has been her partner for two weeks; Offred doesn't know what happened to the previous one but knows not to ask—she knows the answer wouldn't be anything she'd want to hear.

Underlining the women's sense of imprisonment, Offred notes the barriers, floodlights, and men with machine guns on both sides of the road. She and Ofglen go through a checkpoint, where two young men check their identification.

While checking Ofglen's and Offred's passes, one of the young Guardians peeks at Offred's face, and she helps him to see it, tilting her head. The Guardian blushes, and Offred thrills at this small, undetectable act of defiance. She fantasizes about coming back at night and disrobing in front of him, feeling a sense of her power from this fantasy. The Guardians must be sex-starved, she decides, but she also knows that fear keeps them in check, just as it does the Handmaids. Nonetheless, when the young Guardians wave the women through, Offred flaunts her hips as she walks, in a gesture that she finds analogous to thumbing her nose at them.

Chapter 5 features Offred walking with Ofglen along the streets of Cambridge, Massachusetts, the heart of the Republic of Gilead. She remembers walking the same streets with Luke, her husband, and dreaming aloud about buying a house and having children.

They stroll past a store called Lilies of the Field, which sells the habits the Handmaids must wear, and Offred remembers that Lilies used to be a movie theater that showed films with strong, independent women, like Katherine Hepburn, and Lauren Bacall. Instead of going into Lilies, though, Offred and Ofglen cross the street to a food store called Milk and Honey (it should be noted that because women aren't allowed to read, the store signs, and the food tokens, have only pictures). Offred notices oranges in the store, a treat hard to come by in this war-torn time. While waiting in paired lines, the Handmaids all steal furtive glances from under their "wings," looking for someone they might know. Offred longs to see her college friend Moira, but doesn't find her, and she notes that Ofglen isn't looking at all.

Two more women enter the store, one of them "vastly pregnant," and this causes a stir among the Handmaids. Offred notes that this pregnant woman's excursion might be a whim, since pregnant women are no longer required to go on walks, but Offred thinks that the woman, most likely, is merely showing off. Leaving the store, she recognizes her as Janine, a former handmaid trainee from the Red Center who she had disliked.

Next, Offred and Ofglen go into All Flesh, but there isn't much meat: "even the Commanders don't have it every day." While the meat gets wrapped in butcher paper, Offred recalls when groceries came in plastic bags. She had shoved them into a cabinet under the sink until they bulged out, much to Luke's annoyance. He had argued with her about the danger they posed to children, and the fragmented, remembered conversation clues readers in, for the first time, to the fact that Offred and Luke had had a daughter. Back outside, the Handmaids pass tourists from Japan. The so-called "short" (hem just below the knee) skirts on the women remind Offred of the clothes she had worn before, and her observations demonstrate to readers how much her perspective has been colored by her indoctrination:

> the legs come out from beneath them, nearly naked in their thin stockings, blatant, the high-heeled shoes with their straps attached to the feet like delicate instruments of torture ... They wear lipstick, red, outlining the damp cavities of their mouths, like scrawls on a washroom wall, of the time before.

Because of the new regime, Offred views a conservative business-suit skirt, as well as stockings, as racy and obscene; she sees women's hair, uncovered, as a sexual stimulant; and she associates lipstick with trashy graffiti. As in the opening chapter, she appears to possess a warped, childlike innocence, but then, while staring at the women, she remembers, "I used to dress like that. That was freedom," demonstrating yet again that Offred's re-programming has, on some level, failed. The Japanese tourists soon approach Offred and Ofglen, asking through an interpreter (who Offred suspects of being an Eye) if they can take a picture. The Handmaids refuse, remembering the words of Aunt Lydia: "To be seen is to be penetrated." It is a subtly satirical contradiction if we remember the Handmaids *must*, in fact, be sexually penetrable if they hope to survive within the Regime.

Offred stares at the pink painted toenails of a Japanese woman in open-toed shoes, remembering what it felt like to apply nail polish herself, and when the tourists ask if the Handmaids are happy, she murmurs, "Yes, we are very happy," not daring to answer any other way.

In **Chapter 6**, on their way home Offred and Ofglen stop to gaze at the outer wall of what had previously been Harvard Yard. The Wall, which is patrolled by Guardians, features six abortionists who have been hanged—victims of a "Men's Salvaging." They all wear doctors' lab coats, have their hands tied in front of them, and have their heads covered by white bags. Offred thinks the bags make the executed look like scarecrows, which, she realizes, is appropriate. They're meant to frighten. But she also thinks how empty the gesture is, since no woman in her right mind would try to terminate a pregnancy in Gilead.

III Night

Chapter 7 finds Offred reveling the freedom she enjoys at night; she asks herself, "Where should I go?" deciding what memory or fantasy to entertain. On this night her memories center on different pre-Gilead versions of womanhood. In the first, her college friend Moira, "in her purple overalls, one dangly earring, the gold fingernail she wore to be eccentric," tries to talk her into going for a beer instead of finishing a paper due the next day. Moira is the voice of bold freedom.

Next, Offred remembers participating in a book-burning with her mother: pornographic magazines are being burned in the name of feminism. One woman hands Offred a magazine to toss into the fire, but instead, Offred stares at a photo of a naked woman hanging from the ceiling by a chain wound around her hands. Because her mother grows upset, however, Offred soon tosses it, too, into the fire, watching "parts of women's bodies, turning to black ash, in the air, before my eyes." Subtly, Atwood suggests that extremist, censorship-friendly feminism was one factor that led to the formation of Gilead.

Finally, Offred tries to remember the time just before her indoctrination. Realizing that there was a gap of time still unaccounted for, she realizes that she must have been drugged, but she remembers asking about her daughter—her own motherhood is a third version of womanhood. Offred is told that she was "unfit," and they show her a photo of her daughter holding the hand of a woman Offred doesn't know. The girl wears a white dress that goes down to the ground, suggesting baptism or communion dress.

At the end of this section, Offred battles with the reality of her situation; she feels she must tell her story, that the very process is keeping her alive. The nature of storytelling implies a listener/audience, which she both hopes for desperately and despairs of, fully aware that no one can hear it. She mentions that she can't write it, leaving readers, at this point, to assume that they're being exposed to her thoughts.

IV Waiting Room

Chapter 8 opens with Ofglen and Offred at the Wall again— this time, they see a priest and two homosexuals—in Guardian uniforms—who had been hanged. When they leave, Ofglen remarks that it is a beautiful May day. Offred responds perfunctorily, but she then remembers that Mayday used to be a distress signal. She recalls Luke once telling her that it comes from the French m'aidez, which means "help me."

When Offred and Ofglen part, Offred notes that her partner hesitates, as if to say more, but she walks away. Offred watches her "like my own reflection, in a mirror from which I am moving away." In Gilead, Offred is made to feel her anonymity, as well as her utter interchangeability with others, often. She has a function, but she is not a person. She is, as she once says, a "womb with two legs."

Nick is polishing the Commander's car in the driveway again and offhandedly asks, "Nice walk?" Offred nods but doesn't answer—interaction is not allowed. Offred finds Serena Joy, the Commander's Wife, sitting in the garden. She recalls, spitefully, that she had stopped singing on Sunday mornings and had begun making speeches about the sanctity of the home, as well as women's place in it. (Offred notes the inherent hypocrisy of this, since, as a public speaker and activist, Serena failed to practice what she preached herself.) Offred recalls watching her on television, "her sprayed hair and her hysteria," with Luke; he thought she was funny, but her earnestness scared Offred, who now thinks, "How furious she must be, now that she's been taken at her word."

Offred brings the groceries to the kitchen table, noting Rita's complaints at her shopping choices likely stem from jealousy at the trips she is able to make outside the home. As she notes the weird normalcy of the ordinary dishtowel Rita wipes her hands on—"Sometimes these flashes of normalcy come at me from the side, like ambushes"—Cora and Rita discuss who will help Offred with her bath, speaking about it as a chore, and as if she weren't there.

On the way to her room, Offred notices the Commander in the hall, looking at her sleeping quarters—a clear violation. When he hears Offred coming, however, he simply nods, steps around her, and goes. Offred reflects on this, wondering whether this breach is a harbinger of something bad or something good for her, and then she asks, "Was he invading? Was he in my room?" These questions expose her sense of violation, and she notes then that by virtue of calling it "my" room—which she previously, consciously refused to do—she is falling prey to old habits and assuming rights that she no longer officially has.

Chapter 9 begins with Offred surrendering to her impulse to claim the room for herself. She explains that three days after her arrival, she began to *slowly* explore the room—unlike the perfunctory, rushed search people used to perform in their hotel rooms. This reminds Offred of how she used to meet Luke in hotel rooms, in the beginning of their relationship, when he "was still in flight from his wife"—an explanation that tells us she married a divorced man.

Offred explores the room in stages, wanting this little bit of excitement to last. At one point, she finds stains on the mattress, evidence "of love or something like it, desire at least." She covers the mattress and lies on it, wishing for Luke to be next to her, thinking that she understands more fully "why the glass in the window is shatterproof, and why they took down the chandelier." With this in mind, she explores the cupboard and finds brass hooks; she knows that someone who wanted to kill herself could use these. Then, however, she kneels on the floor and finds this message scratched, with a pin or a fingernail, onto the wood: *Nolite te bastardes carborundorum*. Offred doesn't know what this means, though she suspects it's Latin and feels joy in its defiance: "It pleases me to know that her taboo message made it through, to at least one other person." Because Offred suffers from the thought that her own "tale" will reach no one, her reception of this coded message gives her hope that it will be unearthed. Happily, Offred tries to imagine the woman who inscribed the message, and she imagines her as Moira.

Offred tries to get information from Rita about her room's previous resident; when Rita asks "which one?" Offred thinks of Moira again and says, "The lively one... The one with freckles." Rita says that she didn't work out, and darkly warns Offred, "What you don't know won't hurt you."

Chapter 10 opens with Offred confessing that she sings songs like "Amazing Grace" and "Heartbreak Hotel" in her head. (Not surprisingly—given her circumstances—she confuses the lyric "Was blind but now I see" with "Was bound, but now am free.")

As she waits in her room, she recollects Moira's "underwhore" party (like a Tupperware party, with lingerie), and the memory is juxtaposed by her recollection of stories she had read in the newspapers just prior to Gilead's rise—about women "bludgeoned to death or mutilated, interfered with," the last phrase clearly an institutionalized euphemism for rape—and how the crimes gradually grew worse and more worrisome. Because the events seemed distant from Offred's own daily life, however, they seemed unreal to her, and as a result, she failed to act, or even suspect anything like the evolution of Gilead. The passage points to her failure to read societal signs and acts as a warning to the reader to always be cognizant and vigilant, and proactive.

From the window, Offred sees Nick open the car door for the gray-haired Commander, and she thinks that if she could spit or throw the pillow out the window, she could hit him. Upon consideration she's surprised by the fact that she doesn't hate the Commander.

In **Chapter 11**, Offred visits the doctor, which occurs every month. A male nurse, armed with a pistol in a shoulder holster, checks her in, and Offred is soon shown into an exam room. There, she disrobes and lies on the table, where "At neck level there's another sheet, suspended from the ceiling. It intersects me so that the doctor will never see my face. He deals with my torso only." She soon hears footsteps and, in spite of the rules, the doctor chats and calls her "honey." After a quick exam, he whispers, "I could help you," and Offred immediately thinks he has information about Luke. Instead, the doctor propositions her, saying that the door is locked, and that many of the commanders are sterile. Offred nearly gasps at this word, since now "There are only women who are fruitful and women who are barren, that's the law." (Again, women are universally blamed, by law, for that over which they have no control, so as to leave males officially blameless. This institutionalized, illogical pattern of blame appears throughout the novel.) Offred is tempted for a moment, knowing her life depends on conceiving a child, but she refuses. The lascivious doctor is disappointed, and Offred tries to leave the impression that she's not upset. She knows he has the power to report false test results and get her sent to the Colonies, so she lets the doctor think that she may be willing next time. He leaves, and her hands shake as she pulls on her clothes, afraid of the choice she now has.

In **Chapter 12**, Offred describes her bathroom at the house, noting again that there is no mirror, no door locks, and no razors; the specter of potential suicide pervades Offred's environment constantly. She admits to the sense of luxury that a bath affords her, including feeling her own hair in her hands again. However, she avoids looking at her naked body, not out of shame or modesty, but because "I don't want to look at something that determines me so completely."

The smell of the soap makes Offred think of her daughter, and how, when her daughter was only eleven months old, a strange woman stole her from the seat of Offred's supermarket cart. The woman, when caught, cried and said that the baby was hers, given to her by the Lord. Offred next thinks that her daughter was five when she was taken away, so she must be eight years old now. Offred knows that her daughter probably believes her mother is dead, and Offred decides that holding to this belief, on both sides, might make things easier.

After the bath, Cora knocks on the bedroom door—which Offred appreciates—and brings in supper. As Offred eats, she thinks of the many who must do without; she's not hungry, out of nervousness about the upcoming ceremony that night, but there's no place to ditch the food.

V Nap

Napping before the ceremony, **Chapter 13** finds Offred ruminating over her time at the Red Center—the required afternoon naps which prepared the Handmaids for the large expanses of empty time that would become their lives. She recalls Moira's coming to the center three weeks after her arrival, and their rendezvous in the bathroom which was ironically made possible by Janine (the pregnant Handmaid Offred saw while shopping). The previous week, Janine had testified to being gang-raped when she was fourteen and having an abortion. The Aunts had led the Handmaids in chanting that it had been Janine's fault, and that she had led the men on; when Janine kneeled before them all, crying, they chanted "Crybaby," like a mantra. Offred felt bad about this, but claims she couldn't act otherwise. On this day of her planned meeting with Moira, Janine testifies that she accepts responsibility for the rape, which is applauded by the Aunts. Offred excuses herself to the restroom, shuts herself into a stall, and sees a pair of red shoes in the next one. Through a hole, she cautiously speaks Moira's name. They just express their mutual desire for a cigarette, but Offred feels deliriously happy nonetheless.

During Offred's nap, she dreams of her attempted escape from Gilead, running through the woods, hearing shots, and covering her daughter's body to protect her. She wonders fleetingly whether Luke could still be alive. The bell rings to awaken Offred then, and she notes, "Of all the dreams this is the worst."

VI Household

Chapter 14 begins with Offred going to the sitting room, where she kneels near the chair "where Serena Joy will shortly enthrone herself." Offred is the first to arrive, followed by Cora and Rita and then Nick; each of them assumes their position, standing behind Offred. Nick stands so close that his boot touches her foot, and she notes, "I feel my shoe soften, blood flows into it, it grows warm, it becomes a skin." In spite of her exhilaration, however, she moves her foot away.

They all hear Serena limping down the stairs and the hall. She takes her place in the chair, and as they wait for the Commander, she clicks on the TV news, an unexpected treat for Offred though she doesn't trust it. They hear an update on the war, a report on how the Eyes have dismantled an underground sect of Quakers (a famously peaceful community, as Atwood well knows), and news of the resettlement of "The Children of Ham," considered by critics to refer to African Americans. This detail reminds readers that it is the *Caucasian* birthrate in Gilead, specifically, that is at zero, so the inherent racial anxiety of the last news is likely in direct response to this "concern."

Serena flips off the TV, and Offred dissociates from her surroundings, channeling herself back to the Saturday morning when she, Luke, and her daughter tried to escape by car. Offred remembers that she and Luke told their daughter that they were going on a picnic, and they packed for one, bringing nothing else—except forged, one-day visas—so as to not raise suspicions. Driving north, likely to Canada, they plan to give the girl a sleeping pill so she won't blow their cover at the border. One thing readers should note in this chapter is the marked absence of the daughter's name; this seems to reinforce the idea of interchangeable, identity-less females in Gilead, but it also underlines the fact that readers never learn the narrator's real name, the name Offred keeps "like something hidden, some treasure I'll come back to dig up, one day"—as a child or a dog does with a "treasure" in its backyard.

In **Chapter 15**, the Commander enters the sitting room, wearing his black uniform. He looks at the assemblage, "as if taking inventory," sits in his leather chair across from the others, and unlocks the bible from its box. Offred notes how the Commander can read it to them, but they cannot read it themselves; for this reason, the scene has the aura of a bedtime story for children. While Offred waits for him to begin, she penetrates the *Commander* with her gaze, reducing him to a winding list of unsavory, sexualized images:

> the stub of himself, his extra, sensitive thumb, his tentacle, his delicate, stalked slug's eye, which extrudes, expands, winces, and shrivels back into himself when touched wrongly, grows big again....

In textual moments like this, Atwood exposes the fury boiling beneath Offred's surface, thus laying the foundation for her eventual, more blatant rebellion.

The Commander reads aloud about Adam and Noah, as well as a verse concerning Rachel and Leah (one of the novel's epigraphs): "Behold my maid, Bilhah. She shall bear upon my knees, that I may also have children by her." This passage, Offred remembers, was read everyday at breakfast to the Handmaids at the Red Center.

Thinking of the Red Center, Offred recalls another bathroom rendezvous with Moira. In adjacent stalls, Moira tells Offred that she intends to feign illness, developing scurvy by hiding her vitamin C pills, and break out. Offred tries to talk her out of it, but Moira continues, saying the two ambulance drivers could be swayed, through sex, to help her. An aunt then comes into the bathroom to rush them out, and the two women touch fingers through the small hole in the stall wall.

The Commander finishes the reading about Leah and

Rachel, and Serena Joy begins to cry, while Offred tries not to laugh. The Commander calls for a moment of silent prayer, and Offred prays, *Nolite te bastardes carborundorum.* She then remembers Moira carried out from the Red Center on a stretcher, as well as the ambulance later returning. Two Aunts drag Moira, who struggles to walk, back inside the Center. They take her to the Science Lab, where the authorities mutilate Moira's feet so badly that she must be carried to classes. Offred notes that for a first offense, they hurt your feet, and for a second, your hands, since these are unrelated to fertility and reproduction, and are, therefore, "not essential."

The Commander clears his throat and ends this portion of the Ceremony.

In **Chapter 16,** the copulation part of the Ceremony occurs. Fully clothed, except for underwear, Offred lies with her eyes closed on Serena Joy's canopy bed. She lies between Serena Joy's legs, her head on the Wife's stomach, with her arms raised so that Serena can hold her hands. (With Serena seated in this position of control, Offred knows that this control will be extended if/when a baby is conceived and born.) Offred's red skirt is hitched up to her waist, and, dissociated once again, she blandly mentions that, "Below it the Commander is fucking." In this moment, she remembers Queen Victoria's advice to a daughter, which provides specific instructions on dissociation: "Close your eyes and think of England." The Commander, meanwhile, performs the act mechanically, joylessly, like the duty that it is. Offred wonders if she'd enjoy it if he were better, then notes, "Kissing is forbidden between us. This makes it bearable. One detaches oneself. One describes." This, of course, repeats the theme of using storytelling as a means of escape, the basis for the "tale" in its entirety.

Finally, the Commander ejaculates, zips up, nods to them, and leaves. Serena Joy orders Offred to go, too, though the Wife is supposed to let her Handmaid rest for ten minutes to improve the chances of conception. Offred leaves without protest, wondering whether she or Serena Joy had the worse experience.

Chapter 17 finds Offred back in her room and missing Luke; she also repeats her name to herself, without, again, revealing it to her readers/listeners.

As Offred thinks yet again that she would like to steal something, she leaves her room to roam around the house. She's tempted to steal a knife from the kitchen, but instead, she approaches the sitting room. She slips in through the open door, lets her eyes adjust to the darkness, and decides to take a wilted daffodil, when she suddenly realizes someone else is in the room. After a whispered warning not to scream, she sees that it's Nick. He asks what she's doing, and when she doesn't answer, he pulls her to him and kisses her. Soon, however, they break away, both aware of the danger. Nick tells Offred he was coming to find her, and his fingers trace her arm beneath her nightgown's sleeve. Offred feels guilty then, wondering if Luke would understand, and then posits that Nick *is* Luke in another body. But she immediately thinks, "Bullshit," thus demonstrating awareness of her own unreliability as the narrator. She knows that she often has to lie to herself in order to survive.

Offred thinks of the bodies hanging on the Wall, feeling anxiety about what she's already done, when Nick tells her that he was coming to give her a message: the Commander wants her to come to his den the next day.

VII Night

In **Chapter 18**, Offred is back in her room, trembling from her encounter with Nick and still ruminating over Luke. Beginning a section by saying, "Here's what I believe," she proceeds to tell us three different versions of Luke in the present. In the first, Luke lies face down in the woods, shot in the head. She hopes the bullet went "through the place where all pictures were, so that there would have been only one flash, of darkness or pain, dull I hope." She also pictures Luke as a ragged prisoner—prematurely aged, tortured, and unaware of what he's accused of. Lastly, there's this possibility: he escaped. He might have made it across the water and taken shelter in a nearby farmhouse, she thinks. He may now be part of the underground, and she may get a message from him anytime, telling her to be patient; that their family will be together again; that he loves her despite all that's happened. Offred says, "It's this message, which may never arrive, that keeps me alive. I believe in the message." Then, however, she says that she believes in all three versions of Luke.

VII Birth Day
In **Chapter 19**, Offred is troubled by dreams of her daughter and mother, but awakens at the sound of the alarm. Seated in her chair for breakfast, she notices the irony of the meal. With her breakfast comes an egg-cup, one which is shaped like a woman's torso in a skirt, and she notices that under the skirt is a second egg being kept warm. Even the food around her takes on an aura of fertility, nurturing, and birth. But as she eats, a siren sounds. She grabs her cloak and runs down the stairs, and the entire household goes out to see the red Birthmobile parked in the driveway. Offred joins three other Handmaids in the van who are sitting on hard benches.

Offred asks who is giving birth, and one Handmaid tells her it's Ofwarren, then hugs her, crying. Secretly, Offred wonders whether Ofwarren will give birth to a baby or an Unbaby with "a pinhead or a snout like a dog's, or two bodies, or a hole in its heart and no arms, or webbed hands and feet?" Offred explains that chemicals and radiation were, in large part, the reason for the increase in mutations. Here, Atwood's environmentalism seeps through her prose, as it does in much of her work; the regime of Gilead evolved, in part, as a result of man's carelessness regarding the environment.

When the Birthmobile stops, armed Guardians herd the Handmaids into the house. An Emerge van, with doctors and equipment, waits in the driveway; now, they are only called upon when absolutely necessary. Aunt Lydia had discussed, with great disdain, what doctors used to do during a delivery, and remarks that now, there's no anesthetic (better for the baby) and women feel the pain that God always intended as their due punishment: "I will greatly multiply thy sorrow and thy conception; in sorrow thou shalt bring forth children."

Again, the idea of pain and punishment for women as always justified is reinforced, this time by biblical precedent.

As Offred ascends the stairs to the house, a blue Birthmobile arrives with the Commanders' Wives.

Chapter 20 begins with the Handmaids inside the house. Offred hears women chanting upstairs, and as she goes by the dining room, she sees a decadent buffet spread for the Wives, who are in the sitting room. Some rub the belly of the Commander's Wife, who lies on the floor in a white nightgown, as if she were the one about to give birth. Offred notes the Commander is gone, per custom, and Janine lies on his king-sized bed in the master bedroom, a Birthing Stool nearby. The Handmaids sit cross-legged on the floor, watching, and Offred remembers Aunt Lydia telling them that other women, in the future, will have an easier time of it. "Because they will have no memories," Offred thinks, "of any other way."

Stirred by thoughts of birth, Offred next recalls the movies the Handmaids watched at the Red Center once a week, including pornographic films with sado-masochistic violence committed against women. According to Aunt Lydia, these films showed what society had become before the regime. Other times, the movies focused on Unwomen—those who were not Wives, Marthas, or Handmaids. Once, Offred had been watching an Unwomen film when she recognized her mother, younger than Offred had ever seen her, marching with a banner that read: "Take back the night." Her mother, a radical feminist, gave birth to Offred at 37, though friends criticized her for being a "pronatalist." Offred remembers her saying, "A man is just a woman's strategy for making other women." Many critics have commented on the cartoonish, extreme brand of feminism practiced by Offred's mother, noting that rather than championing such a figure, Atwood lampoons her, and thus implies that such sloganeering is reductive and inhibits progress rather than promoting it. Though never so feminist as her mother, Offred notes that she still wants her mother back, "But there is no point to it, this wanting."

In **Chapter 21**, Offred notes that the master bedroom has grown hot and noisy; the Handmaids are chanting breathing instructions to Janine. Soon, a Martha arrives with grape Kool-Aid and paper cups—which Offred notes is spiked, something that could only be overlooked at a Birth Day. Offred feels sympathy pains for Janine, who screams; Aunt Elizabeth announces that Janine is "going into transition." Offred knows that this is Janine's second baby, because she remembers her crying at night at the Red Center, as did many of the others—though Janine did it more noisily than the rest. Aunt Elizabeth asks for the lights to be dimmed and orders someone to fetch the Wife. Janine sits in the lower of the two seats on the Birthing Stool, and when the Wife enters—supported by two other Wives, as if the Wife were pregnant, too—she sits in the higher seat, her legs astride Janine. The Handmaids continue to chant, and Aunt Elizabeth kneels to deliver what appears to be a healthy girl. Aunt Elizabeth smiles at the Handmaids, who also smile. Offred recalls giving birth to her own daughter, with Luke beside her bed, holding her hand.

Aunt Elizabeth cleans the child, who cries only a little then stops, and the Handmaids quietly gather about Janine, congratulating her. Meanwhile, the Wives help the Wife from the Birthing Stool to the bed, where she lies down, and they tuck her in. The baby is placed in the Wife's arms, and the other Wives crowd in, shutting out the Handmaids. The Wife names the child Angela, while the Handmaids stand around Janine so that she won't witness this scene. Janine will be permitted to nurse the baby for a few months, and then she will be transferred to a new household. Offred reminds us, though, that Janine's reward is a guarantee that she will never be sent to the Colonies.

As Offred returns to the Birthmobile, a doctor in the Emerge van asks if the baby is all right. She says yes, and as they ride home on the benches, she thinks about how now, after the excitement, she is confronted by her own failure. She tries to telepathically speak to her mother: "You wanted a women's culture. Well, now there is one. It isn't what you meant, but it exists. Be thankful for small mercies."

In **Chapter 22,** Offred reaches the Commander's house in the late afternoon. She goes to her room, exhausted and welcoming solitude, and lies in bed. "I'm too tired to go on with this story," she says. "Here is a different story, a better one. This is the story of what happened to Moira." She learned it, ironically, through Janine, who after admitting her "fault" at being raped had gained the confidence of Aunt Lydia.

Luring Aunt Elizabeth into the bathroom because a toilet had flooded, Moira had taken her hostage using the long, pointed lever from one of the toilets. She forced Aunt Elizabeth to the basement, where they exchanged clothing, tying her with strips of her veil, and reminding her that she could have killed her but chose mercy, slipped past the Angels and disappeared.

Aunt Lydia tells Janine this story to ask her to keep her eyes and ears open, in case others at the Center were involved, but the story spreads from bed to bed that night. The Handmaids are both excited and frightened by the prospect of Moira being loose and Offred notes, "Already we were losing the taste for freedom, already we were finding these walls secure. In the upper reaches of the atmosphere you'd come apart, you'd vaporize, there would be no pressure holding you together." In spite of their fear, Moira became their fantasy.

Chapter 23 opens with Offred still lying in bed, thinking about how her story is a reconstruction, which she ultimately finds to be impossible:

> If I'm ever able to set this down, in any form, even in the form of one voice to another, it will be a reconstruction then, too, at yet another remove. It's impossible to say a thing exactly the way it was, because what you say can never be exact, you always have to leave something out.

Thus, though there is power in language, Offred notes here that it has limitations, too, that can't be overcome.

Abruptly, Offred states that the Commander asked her to kiss him, but immediately back-pedals and says that smaller events occurred to build to that point. This strange, sudden pronouncement about the kiss works to prove her own point about reconstruction.

At nine, Offred walks down the hall "like a child who's been summoned, at school, to the principal's office" for her illegal meeting with the Commander. Offred knocks on the Commander's door, he tells her to enter, and she lets herself in. She looks around the den, noticing the shelves and shelves of books, and sees the Commander standing by the fireplace mantel. He tells Offred to close the door, then says "hello," which Offred notes is "the old form of greeting," a word she hasn't heard in years.

They sit opposite each other, with a desk between them. For a few minutes, the Commander tries to tell Offred the reason for the meeting, but he doesn't get to the point. Finally, he asks her to play a game of Scrabble, and even though she wants to laugh at the silliness of this request, she manages to maintain her composure. But playing the game awakes in Offred a sensual lust for language: "I hold the glossy counters with smooth edges, finger the letters. The feeling is voluptuous... I would like to take them into my mouth." Here, readers get a literal image of Offred longing to taste words in her mouth again, a textual moment that many critics have noted and discussed as representative of Offred's dependence on language for power and self-construction. Offred and the Commander play two rounds; Offred wins the first and lets the Commander win the second. Then the Commander tells Offred that it's time for her to "go home," meaning back to her room. He thanks her and asks her to kiss him; Offred immediately imagines staging an escape like Moira's. Then, however, she admits that she may not have actually thought this at the time, but inserted it in later, again drawing attention to the fact that this is, at best, a faulty reconstruction.

Offred responds to the Commander's request for a kiss, but he makes her do it again, as if she meant it. Offred concludes by saying, "He was so sad. That is a reconstruction, too." With this last statement, readers feel compelled to take everything with a grain of salt.

IX Night

In **Chapter 24,** Offred goes back in her room, then sits, fully clothed, in a chair in the dark, considering her new situation: she is now in a position to ask for something.

She also tries to analyze the Commander, who doesn't act like the "sex machine" Aunt Lydia told her all men are, but feels there's something strange about the whole setup. This reminds Offred of a TV documentary she'd seen as a child, about "one of those wars." In the film, one interviewee had been the mistress of a man who supervised a camp where Jews were killed in ovens. Offred, with a young mind full of fairy tales, had the impression that people had been eaten, as in "Hansel and Gretel." (Many critics have addressed how cannibalism, and mutilation, have played a part in Atwood's work, particularly in relation to the archetypal myths and fairy tales to which she often alludes.) In the film, the mistress denied knowing about the ovens and insisted that the man had not been a monster. Considering this, Offred decides that a humanity can be "invented" for anyone. In this case, Offred thinks, "Probably he had some endearing trait: he whistled, off-key, in the shower, he had a yen for truffles, he called his dog Liebchen and made it sit up for little pieces of raw steak." But Offred then recalls that the mistress killed herself a few days after the interview.

Offred prepares to undress, but then she feels a sudden, volcanic eruption of laughter roiling within her; she must stay quiet, however. She covers both hands over her mouth, drops to her knees, and crawls into the cupboard. She stifles her laugh in her cloak, and when the fit passes, she fingers the scratched Latin phrase with her fingers. In this moment, Offred cynically thinks, "Why did she write it, why did she bother? There's no way out of here."

X Soul Scrolls

In **Chapter 25**, the crash of a dropped breakfast tray and Cora's scream wake Offred the next morning, when Cora finds Offred sleeping beneath her cloak in the cupboard. Cora thought that

Offred had run off or killed herself; fumbling for an excuse, Offred says that she must have fainted, but this only leads Cora to believe that Offred's pregnant. In a compromise that surprises Offred, they decide to lie about the spilled food: that way, the Marthas will not have to answer for another breakfast.

Offred announces that this scene with Cora occurred in May, and that it is now summer. Commenting on the "female shapes" of the new flowers, she states: "There is something subversive about this garden of Serena's, a sense of buried things bursting upwards ... to say: Whatever is silenced will clamor to be heard, though silently." A decidedly female space, the garden reinforces not only Atwood's environmentalist idealism, but also offers a sensuality for these women that is otherwise now denied them by Gilead's theocracy.

Offred tells readers that she and the Commander have an arrangement: she meets him after dinner, in the den, two or three times a week, the chauffeur Nick's hat askew or missing is her signal. As for the reason for the visits, she has concluded that "his motives and desires [aren't] obvious even to [the Commander]." During their second visit, after Scrabble the Commander pulls out a gift for Offred: an issue of *Vogue* from the 1970s. As he dangles this "bait," Offred is surprised by how much she wants it, since she'd only read such magazines on planes and in doctors' waiting rooms. But as she considers the allure of women's magazines, she realizes that they always promised transformation, possibilities, and immortality. Nonetheless, Offred hesitates, wondering if this is all a test, and says, "It's not permitted." The Commander tells her, "In here, it is." Realizing that the bigger taboo is meeting the Commander at all, Offred takes the magazine from him; however, she soon grows uncomfortable when she realizes that the Commander is intently watching her read the magazine. Suddenly, she asks him why, and how, he has this magazine, since all of them were believed to have been destroyed. The Commander vaguely answers, saying that he appreciates "old things." Offred then asks why he decided to show the magazine to her, and he responds, "Who else could I show it to?" When she suggests his wife, he confesses that she doesn't talk to him much anymore, and that they no longer seem to have much in common. And in this moment, Offred realizes what the Commander wants from these visits: understanding. "It was too banal to be true," she says.

On her third visit, Offred asks the Commander for hand lotion, which he promises to get her as long as she doesn't use it around Serena Joy—a subtle allusion to the Ceremony. When he brings it for her at the fourth visit, they agree to stash it in the den. This need for secrecy comes as a surprise to the Commander, who as Offred tells him in anger, thinking of the reason many objects (razor blades, glass) aren't available to Handmaids, "ought to know."

In **Chapter 26**, Offred notices a new awkwardness surrounding the next Ceremony. Before, the ritual had been an "unpleasant job," wherein she (and she suspects, the Commander) would "pretend not to be present ... existing apart from the body." She feels suddenly shy and uncomfortably senses the Commander's eyes on her, conscious and ashamed of her hairy legs and armpits, thus indicating that the Commander was no longer "a thing" to her. She feels a mixture of guilt that "our functions were no longer as separate as they should have been in theory," and a pleasing power over Serena Joy. Critic Joyce Wexler posits that in this chapter, Offred's testimony begins to sound like confession.

> The narrator confesses to her own complicity in adapting to the new order.... Rather than sacrifice her life in a futile gesture of rebellion, she begins to exploit the meager advantages of her position.... She commits the sin of adjusting to an unjust order.

But even the path of complicity is fraught with danger for Offred, and she moves her head when the Commander reaches up, seemingly to touch her face. When they speak of it afterward, his explanation is that he finds the Ceremony "impersonal." Offred sarcastically asks him, "How long did it take you to find that out?" explaining to readers, "You can see from the way I was speaking to him that we were already on different terms." In this passage, as well as the earlier scene in which Offred loses her temper with him, readers see she's reclaimed language and her voice, and this restores to Offred some of the power she'd previously lost.

She considers Aunt Lydia's statement that in the future, when the population level is healthier, "we'll no longer have to transfer you from one house to another because there will be enough to go round. There can be bonds of real affection." Offred realizes that as a result of the secret Scrabble meetings, she has already, in an unacknowledged way, been re-defined as a mistress, "provide [in] what is otherwise lacking." She's afraid that Serena Joy knows or has put the Commander up to it to rid herself of him, thus achieving "her version of freedom." Regardless, Offred is happier than before, enjoying the intellectual engagement that now fills hours previously spent doing nothing, and aware that she is now of more value to the Commander, "no longer merely a usable body."

At the beginning of **Chapter 27**, Offred walks, in hot, humid weather, with Ofglen, shopping baskets on their arms. They visit the wall, where she is disturbed by the lack of "criminals": "When I can see the bodies, the actual bodies, when I can guess from the sizes and shapes that none of them is Luke, I can believe also that he is still alive." She remembers the ice-cream shop of pre-Gilead where she used to take her daughter, and the ironic use for the old lingerie shop, which now houses Soul Scrolls, where prayers for health, wealth, a death, a birth, or a sin are printed out, and spoken by, machines for a cost.

As the two women stand in front of Soul Scrolls, looking through the glass, Offred catches Ofglen's gaze in the window, watching her. They see each other's eyes, and Offred says "Now it's hard to look away. There's a shock in this seeing: it's like seeing somebody naked, for the first time. There is risk, suddenly, in the air between us, where there was none before." As they both experience this sensation, Ofglen gathers the courage to ask a blasphemous question: "Do you think God listens to these machines?" Knowing the question is treasonous, Offred considers screaming, running away, or turning away without a word, but instead, she replies, "No."

Ofglen sighs in relief, and the two talk comfortably, familiarly, for a moment, considering the safety of the location for casual discussion. Soon, however, they turn and walk back to the checkpoint, still whispering. Offred feels elated, but when Ofglen says that Offred can "join us," she worries that Ofglen is a spy who's setting a trap for her, saying "such is the soil in which we grow." That is, because of the regime, everyone fears placing trust in anyone or anything. Nonetheless, Offred wants to ask about Moira, Luke, her mother, and her daughter, but she can't, because they are fast-approaching the main street.

Suddenly, then, a black van, belonging to the Eyes, cruises toward them. Offred immediately thinks that microphones picked up their conversation, but when the van stops right in front of them, and two Eyes jump out, they grab a man walking on the street; they beat him and throw him in the back of the van, slamming the door shut. Offred admits, "What I feel is relief. It wasn't me."

In **Chapter 28**, Offred is too excited to sleep, so she sits at the window, feeling the white, sheer curtain shroud her face and body. In her room, she has a small, electric fan, and she thinks that if she were Moira, she'd take it apart, "reduce it to its cutting edges," but then Offred notes, with regret, "I'm not Moira." With her lopsided "old school" branch of lesbian feminism, Moira, she thinks, would surely disapprove of the Commander the same way she disapproved of Luke, since he was a married man. Offred remembers, the argument, which took place in Offred's kitchen, in a rundown apartment she had when both she and Moira were in their early twenties. She worked a computer at an insurance company, so a hotel room rendezvous with Luke had offered an escape from a depressing apartment and job. They argue the point further, until Moira notes, "We sound like your mother," and they both laugh. Offred concludes "She was my oldest friend. Is," revising past to present tense again, as she does throughout the narrative— in reference to Luke, her daughter, her mother, and Moira— revealing a consistent undercurrent of hope.

Offred later moved into a better apartment and got a new job, wherein she transcribed books onto computer discs. It's strange, Offred thinks, to remember how women had jobs, just as it was strange to remember paper money having value. In retrospect, she realizes that the lack of "portable money," and the propensity of electronic transactions, made the regime change possible. She remembers the president and Congress being shot, and how the army initially blamed Islamic fanatics. The entire government was gone, and the Constitution was (supposedly) temporarily suspended. Offred notes that there wasn't rioting; rather, everyone stayed home watching television, looking for direction when there was no enemy in sight. On the phone, Moira had told Offred, "Here it comes." Slowly but purposefully, newspapers were censored or closed, roadblocks and identipasses appeared, and Pornomarts and Feels on Wheels shut down.

Offred tells us that at this time, she and Luke had been married for a few years, and that their daughter was three or four years old. She recalls the surprise she felt the day she could no longer use her Compucard to buy cigarettes, and how that same afternoon at work, her boss told the women that he was required, by law, to let them go. The women tried to argue with him, but when Offred looked into the corridor behind him, she saw two men, in uniform, with machine guns. The women left but lingered outside, on the library steps, numb with shock. Offred sensed a pervasive guilt: "What was it about this that made us feel we deserved it?"

She returned home, but no one was there, so she wandered from room to room, touching things. She phoned the bank without success, and Moira came over and informed her, "they" froze all F—rather than M—bank accounts: "All they needed to do is push a few buttons. We're cut off." She also told Offred women couldn't hold property anymore, and Offred notes that Moira seemed gleeful, "as if this was what she'd been expecting for some time and now she'd been proven right." Moira suggested that Offred transfer her funds to Luke, while she herself planned to go "underground." Finally, Moira noted that "they" had to cut off women's Compucounts and jobs at the same time: "Can you picture the airports otherwise? They don't want us going anywhere, you can bet on that," she said.

Later, Offred picked up her daughter from school, and Luke came home and tried to comfort his wife. However, when he said, "You know I'll always take care of you," Offred felt he was patronizing her, then wondered if she was simply paranoid. Though there were protest marches, they stopped completely when the authorities opened fire on marchers. Offred didn't march, because Luke said she had to think about her family, and she started doing more housework and baking, trying not to cry during meals: "By this time I'd started to cry, without warning, and to sit beside the bedroom window, staring out."

Offred hears someone leaving the house and soon sees that it's Nick, to whom she hasn't spoken since the night they kissed. His cap is sideways, a signal for her, and she wonders what he gets in return for his participation in the scheme, half suspecting he will turn her in.

She has a final recollection: the night she lost her job, Offred refused to make love to Luke, suspecting that he didn't mind the new arrangements. In retrospect, she feels her suspicion was unjust and untrue, and yet at chapter's end, she directly addresses Luke to ask, "Was I right?" They had never spoken of it, because Offred grew too afraid to ask.

In **Chapter 29**, Offred sits across from the Commander in his office, noting the now-informal tone of their meetings. Her shoes are off, and her legs are tucked up beneath her. She describes how things look by firelight, and then she says, "I add the firelight in," reminding readers yet again that she can add and subtract as she tells the story, emphasizing her power as the storyteller as well as her unreliability. Though she has read magazines and is halfway through *Hard Times*, she feels vulnerable when he watches her, and suggests they talk instead. Eventually, she works up the courage to ask him what *Nolite te bastardes carborundorum* means, and after she struggles with the pronunciation, she offers to write it down for him. After hesitating, he pushes his pen across the desk, along with a notepad. As Offred writes, she feels the power of words in the pen; Aunt Lydia had taught the handmaids that "Pen is Envy" (critics note the wordplay with Freud's "penis envy"). Here, the power of language through writing is, for a moment, restored to Offred, giving her one more medium through which to construct herself.

When she finishes writing, the Commander smiles and explains that it's the kind of warped Latin that prep school boys throw around as a joke. He pulls down an old textbook and shows her a hand-written message that Offred recognizes as the one in her cupboard. The phrase, the Commander tells her, means "don't let the bastards grind you down." Offred quickly realizes that her predecessor must have learned the phrase in the same room, doing precisely what Offred does now. She asks what happened to the former Handmaid, and the Commander explains, matter-of-factly, that she hanged herself. Serena had found out. Offred asks what she used to do it, and when he avoids answering, she thinks, "Torn bedsheet, I figure. I've considered the possibilities." Offred guesses that it was Cora who found the body, then suggests that perhaps she should stop these visits. Under the transparent guise of concern for her enjoyment, the Commander convinces her not to stop, but she feels now that she has something on him now: the possibility of her own death, and his guilt. And when he asks what she would like, besides lotion, she tells him she wants to know what's going on.

XI Night

In **Chapter 30**, Offred sees Nick outside in the shadows, and thinks about how people can't replace each other (i.e., Nick for Luke), and how Moira said that even though "you can't help what you feel, ... you can help how you behave." Offred dismisses this and says, once again, "Context is all," thus implying that perhaps under normal circumstances, Moira's philosophy applies; however, Offred no longer lives in a world of free will.

Offred next recalls the night before she, Luke, and her daughter try to escape; Luke had the difficult task of "taking care" of the cat, whose unfed presence could give them away. Bitterly, Offred notes that killing the cat hadn't mattered in the end, and she wonders who reported them. Regardless, the Eyes had been ready for them, and Offred says that the moment a betrayal is exposed is the worst—that flash when a person realizes "that some other human being has wished you that much evil."

Offred tries then to remember what Luke and her daughter looked like, but she finds it more and more difficult. She decides to say her prayers, though they won't be performed as they were at the Red Center. She offers a deconstructionist Lord's Prayer with personal asides: she wants to know God's real name (as readers want to know *hers*), but just as she views her narrative as a letter beginning *Dear You*, she decides that "You" will have to suffice; she expresses doubt that what's happening is what "You" intended; the daily bread isn't a problem, and she isn't worried about her own forgiveness, but she wants her loved ones to be safe, or if they have to die, she wishes for their deaths to be swift; she says she'll try to forgive those responsible for her circumstances, though it's hard; she considers temptation, remembering that Aunt Lydia used to say, "What you don't know won't tempt you" (and here, Atwood seems to hint that Gilead is an attempt to reverse the consequences of the Fall); her temptation lies in the hooks, from which she knows that she could hang herself; and she concludes by saying that she feels as if she's talking to a wall, and asks "How can I keep on living?"

XII Jezebel's

It's summer in **Chapter 31**, a time for lighter clothes and uncomfortably hot nights—nights that nearly inspire Offred to scratch off days on her wall, though she knows she's not serving a jail sentence.

On their walk, Offred and Ofglen see two bodies hanging on the Wall. One is a Catholic, though not a priest, while one simply has a red "J" on it. This doesn't refer to Jews, Offred knows, because they're denoted with a yellow star; besides, because they were declared "Sons of Jacob," they all had the option to emigrate to Israel or convert. Offred ultimately decides that whatever the "J" stood for, the man on the Wall is "just as dead."

Offred and Ofglen walk across an open space to talk, though it's "amputated speech," and make their way toward a park with an old, Victorian building, once called Memorial Hall. While the two women look at the building, Ofglen tells Offred that there's a password, used to determine who is in the underground: Mayday.

When Offred comes home, she sees Nick with his hat askew, but he doesn't look at her, and he immediately turns and goes in once he knows that she's seen him. Serena Joy, meanwhile, sits under the willow tree, knitting and smoking. Offred keeps her eyes down and tries to slip past, but the Wife summons her and asks her to hold her wool, a confining position. Serena Joy confirms that Offred hasn't yet conceived a child and reminds her that time is running out. Offred is shocked, however, when Serena Joy suggests that perhaps the Commander can't father a child; according to law, it is only women "who remain stubbornly closed, damaged, defective." Nonetheless, Offred admits that it's possible, and she and Serena Joy look each other in the eye for the first time. Serena suggests that they try another man, though Offred reminds her that this is against the law. Dismissing this objection, Serena tells Offred that it's done often, and in fact, Ofwarren (Janine) had been impregnated by a doctor; Offred rejects this option, however. Serena agrees, wanting someone they could trust, adding, "I was thinking of Nick." The Commander will be kept out of the arrangement, they decide, and after Offred accepts the proposal, Serena Joy tells her that she may be able to get something for her: a photograph of her daughter. Offred feels furious, discovering that Serena knew all along where her daughter was placed and didn't say a word, but she is so desperate to see her daughter that she's stunned into silence. As a parting gift, Serena Joy places a cigarette that she's struggled to light into Offred's hand, telling her that she can get a match from Rita in the kitchen.

In **Chapter 32**, Offred brings the groceries into the kitchen and asks Rita for a match, adding that Serena Joy said it's OK. Rita gives it grudgingly and Offred hurries upstairs with her cigarette, thinking that it's been so long that it could make her sick. She considers smoking it in the bathroom with the water running, or by the open window of her room, but then she thinks about flushing it down the toilet, or consuming it orally over a long time so that she could keep, and hide, the match in her mattress. She thinks, "I could burn the house down. Such a fine thought, it makes me shiver."

The night before, the Commander drank, which he now does often around Offred. He doesn't offer her any drinks, of course—"we both know what my body is for." Sometimes, Offred notes, he gets silly when he drinks; making up nonsense words at Scrabble, or sitting on the floor beside her chair, holding her hand. This small-scale reversal makes Offred recall Ofglen's words regarding the Commander: "He's way up there. He's at the top, and I mean the very top." Offred finds this hard to imagine in such moments.

The Commander talks to Offred often, ranging from being querulous to philosophical, but oftentimes, he tries to justify himself, his part in the regime. He explains to Offred that the main problem lay not with the women, but the men: "There was nothing for them to do with women," he claims. Offred, confused, says that there was access to porn and prostitution, but the Commanders says that the issue wasn't sex, which was easy and available for purchase. "There was nothing to work for, nothing to fight for," he said, explaining that what men complained of most was an "inability to feel." Offred asks if they feel now, and the Commander says "yes," then comes around to stand behind her, his hands on her shoulders, and asks her what she thinks. She tries to evade the question, but when she tells him that she has no opinion, she notes, "He knows what I think, all right." The Commander explains that their intentions had been to make things better, but he admits that "Better never means better for everyone ... It always means worse for some."

Chapter 33 opens with Offred and Ofglen walking, in the late afternoon, toward a modern-looking building with a banner that reads, "WOMEN'S PRAYVAGANZA TODAY." Offred notes the Guardians with machine guns flanking the doorway, ready for "whatever dangerous or subversive acts they think we might commit inside." The event will take place in a covered courtyard, where there are assigned areas for

Handmaids and Wives, as well as a gallery for "lower-ranking women" like Econowives and Marthas. The Handmaids file into an area with no chairs that is cordoned off by a scarlet rope, thus forming a kind of "corral or pen." Ofglen tells Offred to head to the back, where they can speak more freely; during a televised event like this, it would be hard to signal someone out. The two women kneel down, and Ofglen nudges Offred so that she notices Janine, paired with a new woman. She must have been transferred, and Offred wonders: Was something wrong with her breast-milk? Was there a fight over the baby? Ofglen soon tells Offred, however, that the baby turned out to be a "shredder," and the news makes Offred feel nauseated. This was Janine's second miscarriage, Ofglen notes, and Janine thinks it's her fault, "for being sinful. She used a doctor, they say ..." This is no surprise to Offred, of course, but she thinks, "It's like Janine, though, to take it upon herself."

Offred next recalls how one morning, at the Red Center, when everyone else was getting dressed, Janine just sat in her nightgown on the edge of her bed, whispering nonsense to herself from her pre-Gilead days as a waitress: "Can I get you some coffee to begin with?" It was Moira who shook her out of it finally, reminding her of life in the Colonies, saying, "You can't stay *there*, you aren't *there* anymore. That's all gone." Moira convinces her to start getting dressed, and tells Offred that if Janine does that again, when Moira isn't around, "you just have to slap her like that." Offred now realizes, of course, that Moira gave these instructions because she was planning her escape.

Back at the Prayvaganza, in **Chapter 34**, the Commander in charge of the service enters. He looks impressive, Offred reluctantly admits, so she kills this seed of admiration by imagining him in bed with his Handmaid and wife "fertilizing away like mad, like a rutting salmon." He approaches the podium, speaks of victory and sacrifice (which Offred tunes out), and leads the women in prayer and a hymn ("There is a Balm in Gilead"). Twenty Angels march into the space, and twenty veiled daughters, dressed in white, come forward: "The marriages are of course arranged." Offred wonders if they're old enough to remember what life had been like before; even the fourteen year olds should, she thinks, but in a few years, "They'll have always have been in white, in groups of girls; they'll always have been silent."

The Commander had once told Offred, "We've given them more than we've taken away," citing the now-extinct humiliations of singles bars, blind dates, and plastic surgery. She remembers his argument, which, *theoretically*, sounds sympathetic and reasonable: unattractive women can have a man, too ("nobody's left out"); men can no longer leave a single mother to struggle alone on welfare; men can't beat women any longer; and people now respect mothers. "What did we overlook?" the Commander asks Offred. "Falling in love," she responds. He also notes that historically speaking, the idea of "falling in love" is an anomaly, and that the Regime simply returned things "to Nature's norm."

After some words from the Commander doing the presentation on women's roles, the ceremony ends and they're "doing the rings, lifting the veils." Offred thinks, bitterly, about how the Angels will qualify for a Handmaid later, if their wives can't conceive, but how the wives are stuck for life. She imagines the clumsy sexual fumblings of the new grooms before her. When she leaves the ceremony, Ofglen whispers, "We know you're seeing him alone." Ofglen wants to know what he wants: "Kinky sex?" Offred lets her think that's what it is, and Ofglen tells her to use the visits to find out anything she can.

Chapter 35 opens with Offred thinking again of her and Luke's failed escape. At the border, the guard goes inside with their passports; Luke gets out of the car, as if to stretch his legs, while Offred lights a cigarette, their daughter sleeping among stuffed animals in the back-seat. Suddenly, though, Luke rushes back, puts the key in the ignition and throws the car into reverse. He says that the guard had picked up the phone, and Luke drives fast to a dirt road, then the woods. They all leave the car and run, and Offred says, "I don't want to be telling this story." She realizes, of course, that she doesn't have to, then thinks of the woman who scratched the Latin phrase into the cupboard. "Fat lot of good it did her," she thinks. "Why fight?"

Next, Offred considers how the Commander addressed and dismissed the issue of falling in love, and states her own opinion on the topic: "it was the way you understood yourself." Offred reflects, in depth, on the complexities of love, and on how, without even realizing it, "I love you" becomes "*I loved you*, and the tense would be past, and you would be filled with a sense of wonder, because it was such an amazing and precarious and dumb thing to have done." Thinking again that Luke might be dead, she recalls how a package, containing a dead soldier's belongings, used to be delivered to a loved one; she notes that Luke *was* a loved one, but then she angrily chastises herself, editing her own story once again: "*Is, is*, only two letters, you stupid shit, can't you manage to remember it, even a short word like that?" Offred weeps, thinking herself a lady in waiting (which is what they used to call maternity clothing stores, she adds) as well as "a blank, here, between parentheses," reiterating how her very being is constructed by virtue of language. Soon, though, Serena Joy knocks on Offred's door and hands her a Polaroid. Her daughter is tall now, standing in a white dress. Offred thinks, "I have been obliterated for her ... A shadow of a shadow, as dead mothers become. You can see it in her eyes. I am not there." Offred can't bear feeling erased and regrets Serena Joy bringing her the photo at all.

At the beginning of **Chapter 36,** the Commander is drunk before Offred even gets to his room. After she arrives, he tells her, as he might a child, that he has a surprise for her and playfully makes her guess. When he brings the items from behind his back, she explains, "It's a garment, apparently, and for a woman: there are the cups for the breasts, covered in purple sequins. The sequins are tiny stars"—a black market item. She wonders if the kinky side of him is finally surfacing when he tells her that it's a disguise, and that she'll need to wear make-up also; he wants to take her out. Still shy in front of the Commander, though, she changes into the gaudy outfit while his back is turned. The Commander holds up a small mirror from Serena Joy's room while she applies lipstick and eyeliner, also procured by him. Next, he gives her a Wife's blue cloak, and after she pulls up the hood, they head out, holding hands while Nick drives them through the twilight. Looking at the back of Nick's head, she feels his disapproval of her; when he opens the door for her to get in, she tries to catch his eye, but he doesn't look.

They go through two checkpoints without a problem, but then the Commander asks Offred to get down on the floor; they have to drive through a gateway, past which Wives aren't allowed. They clear this checkpoint also, and when they finally arrive, the Commander tells Offred to leave the cloak with Nick, and tells Nick "On the hour, as usual." Offred realizes then that "this, too, is something he's done before." When the couple exits the car, Nick finally looks at her, but she can't detect whether his face registers contempt or indifference. Offred and the Commander stand in an alleyway, then walk down a bleak corridor, where the Commander puts a purple tag on Offred's wrist and tells her that if anyone asks, she's "an evening rental."

As **Chapter 37** begins, Offred and the Commander continue down another corridor, where Offred notices numbers on the doors and recognizes the place as a hotel she and Luke once used. Now, it's full of lounging, made-up women, wearing garish, spangled outfits like Offred's, or old-fashioned lingerie, or swimsuits, or workout clothes, or cheerleader uniforms; they are surrounded by men in dark uniforms and suits. The Commander says that this feels like walking into the past, but Offred wonders if the past was ever actually like this: "A movie about the past is not the same thing as the past," she thinks.

Later, as they make the rounds, Offred realizes that the Commander is showing *her* off while, at the same time, showing off *for her*. After all, she, as a Handmaid, should not be in this place, and the Commander is enjoying breaking the rules: "It's a juvenile display, the whole act, and pathetic; but it's something I understand," Offred notes. He eventually sits her down on a sofa and asks her what she thinks of the club, and she answers, "I thought this sort of thing was strictly forbidden." The Commander says it is, officially, but that nature can't be cheated, and men, by design, need variety, "part of the procreational strategy." She asks who the people at the club are; he assumes she means the men, but when she clarifies that she meant to ask about the women, he explains that many were prostitutes, though there are a few professionals, too: a lawyer, a sociologist, a business executive. Soon, he leaves to get her a drink, and as she looks around, she spots Moira.

Dressed in a ragged, old black Playboy bunny costume, Moira smokes and talks to a woman in a devil costume, but eventually, as she looks around, her eyes "snag on" Offred; she motions with her head and holds up a hand with all five fingers spread out. It's their old signal; they'll meet in the washroom in five minutes. The Commander soon comes back with their drinks, and Offred asks about the restroom. He gives her directions and advises her to show the tag on her wrist if she gets stopped.

In **Chapter 38**, Offred finds the restroom entrance, where an Aunt armed with a cattle prod tells her she has fifteen minutes. Moira and Offred kid each other about their costumes, but then Offred starts to cry. Moira makes room on the couch and they both sit, taking off their shoes. Offred explains then that the Commander smuggled her into the club and, noting they have little time, asks Moira to tell how she became a regular at Jezebel's.

Here, Offred inserts a kind of apologia for her own editing choices—the story Moira is about to recount was told during the course of two bathroom breaks, and recreated in her voice. Here, once again, Offred draws attention to the fact that the storytelling is, by definition, subjective, altered through the lens of the teller. Not only does Offred construct herself, she constructs Moira and everyone else through this filter.

Moira appears to start narrating the account of her escape, though we know that what we're reading is merely Offred's impressionistic account of Moira's story. Moira begins with leaving Aunt Elizabeth tied up to the furnace. She leaves the Center with no plan; she knows that the women she had known at her former job at a feminist press had been arrested, so she just heads north, making her way through checkpoints and barriers. She finally decides to go to the address of a Quaker couple who had been part of the mailing list she memorized when the press was in danger. When the woman comes to the door, Moira says that she's doing a questionnaire, but once she's inside the house, she explains her real identity. They are sympathetic, and burn Aunt Elizabeth's clothing and pass before handing her off to another house on the "Underground Femaleroad." Moira deeply feels the weight of people risking their lives in order to help her during the eight or nine months she spends underground. She makes it up to Maine in a truck full of chickens, and the plan is then to get Moira across the border by boat; however, the authorities pick up Moira and her helpers, an old fisher couple, as they are heading down to the dock. In the back of a van, Moira thinks she'll be killed or returned to the Center, and she considers killing herself but can't, since there are two guards watching her. She is eventually given a choice: Jezebel's or the Colonies. Moira explains the advantages of the club, including face cream, decent food, drugs, and only working nights. Offred, alarmed by the Moira's resignation, thinks, "I don't want her to be like me. Give in, go along, save her skin." Moira lightens the mood, then, hinting that she now gets to enjoy sex with other women again, which the club not only allows but encourages.

At chapter's end, Offred reflects on her struggle as narrator; the story she *wants* to tell isn't aligned with the truth:

> Here is what I'd like to tell. I'd like to tell a story about how Moira escaped, for good this time. Or if I couldn't tell that, I'd like to say she blew up Jezebel's, with fifty Commanders inside it. I'd like her to end with something daring and spectacular, some outrage, something that would befit her. But as far as I know that didn't happen. I don't know how she ended, or even if she did, because I never saw her again.

Readers are reminded here that Offred's textual constructions, of herself and others, may be misleading, since she sometimes sees and imagines what she merely *desires* to be true.

In **Chapter 39**, the Commander and Offred take the elevator up to a room, which Offred recognizes from before, "once upon a time." (This small allusion indicates that this is a fairy tale turned upside down, into a nightmare.) To stall, she goes into the bathroom, where she remembers Moira saying that she saw Offred's mother in one of the Colonies films. When Offred says she thought her mother dead, Moira responds: "You should wish it for her." Offred then tries to recall the last time she saw her mother, and remembers when she and Luke discovered her mother had been taken from her apartment, with signs of a struggle. Offred wants to call the police, but Luke talks her out of it. Offred thinks that her mother will think of something to survive, but she knows this isn't true.

She forces herself back to the present moment, in the hotel bathroom. Her makeup is a mess, and she thinks about how she must get back to the house by midnight (another fairy tale reference); the Ceremony is the next day, and Serena will want Offred "serviced" by Nick that evening. Soon, she goes out and lies beside the Commander on the king-size bed. Referring to the next day's Ceremony, he says, "I thought we could jump the gun." Ruffled, she asks him why he brought her to the hotel. He stumbles to answer her question—he thought she'd like a change, then it's an experiment—he finally says, "You said you wanted to know." He begins to undress, and Offred wonders if sex will be even worse this way. He undresses her, but she lies there "like a dead bird." Disappointed with her response, the Commander offers to turn out the lights, and Offred explains, "The trouble is that I can't be, with him, any different from the way I usually am with him." She makes herself fake it in order to get it over with.

XIII Night
In **Chapter 40**, it is midnight and Offred, back in her red "habit" and her room, finds the pre-storm heat oppressive. As planned, Serena Joy comes for her, and they both creep down the stairs and through the kitchen, where Serena Joy tells Offred how to get to Nick's front door; she'll stay in the kitchen as a lookout. Thunder brews outside as she reaches the garage, only steps away; she enters, goes up the stairs, and thinks about how this apartment must have once been for a

student or a young, single person with a job. After she knocks, Nick opens the door, and she sees his sparsely furnished, monastic room; "No pictures on the walls, no plants. He's camping out." He steps aside to let her pass, and then there are no preliminaries; he doesn't speak, but turns off the lamp, undresses her, and kisses her body until "I'm alive in my skin, again."

Offred then says, however, that she made this up. "Here is what happened," she says. After arriving, Nick offers Offred a drag off his cigarette, which she accepts. He looks at her but doesn't speak, which makes her feel uncomfortable, stupid, and ugly. Awkwardly, she finally speaks up: "I don't have much time." Without smiling, Nick responds, "I could just squirt it into a bottle and you could pour it in." This makes Offred think that Nick, too, feels used, so she tries to appeal to his humanity. The two then jokingly exchange cliché pick-up lines from old movies—"an acknowledgment that that we are acting"—which lightens the mood, and Offred thinks that no one probably "ever talked like that in real life." She knows the banter works as a means of insulation, a barrier of protection, and her and Nick's use of it suddenly makes her cry. He comes forward, puts his arms around her, and reminds her they don't have much time. He leads her to the fold-out bed and starts unbuttoning, saying, "No romance ... Okay?" Offred notes that in the past, this meant, "no strings," but now it means "don't risk yourself for me." But there isn't *really* thunder booming outside, Offred confesses; she added that into the story to cover up the noises she made while making love with Nick.

However, Offred then says her tryst with Nick didn't exactly happen this way, either: "All I can hope for is a reconstruction: the way love feels is always only approximate." During sex, she thinks of her betrayal of Luke, which recalls her earlier three versions of his fate: "If I knew for certain he's dead, would that make a difference?"

IX Salvaging
Chapter 41 begins with Offred wishing that her story was different, and that it showed her in a better light. She offers

and apology: "I'm sorry there is so much pain in this story. I'm sorry it's in fragments, like a body caught in crossfire or pulled apart by force. But there is nothing I can do to change it." Of course, the text is a reflection and a symbol of her fragmented, reconstructed identity, which she tries to put back together. By telling her story, she demonstrates a belief in the "you" she is telling it to, and thus believes "you" into being; in the spirit of Descartes' "I think, therefore I am" axiom, she says, "I tell, therefore you are." There is some suggestion that the "you" specifically indicates Luke, however, when she next says that she's coming to a part "you" won't like, "because in it I do not behave well, but I will try nonetheless to leave nothing out."

By saying "This is the story, then"—which we've heard before, only to later learn it's not true—Offred starts to explain that she went back to Nick often, without Serena Joy's knowledge, for her own gratification. After an evening with the Commander, she'd sneak back toward her room but continue to the Marthas' staircase, then down through the kitchen and out the door to Nick's. He opens the door, never expecting or waiting for her, and her never expecting him to be there or let her inside, and she ritually asks him if it's too late, a point of control that makes Offred feel like there's a choice. She comes in after he shakes his head, and then he closes the window and turns off the lamp. She's already half-undressed, and they don't talk until afterward. She notes that with the Commander, she closes her eyes, but with Nick, she keeps them open and wants lights on (though they can't for fear of discovery). She tries to memorize Nick, "save him up so I can live on the image, later." In retrospect, she wishes she had done this with Luke, who is fading day by day in her memory, as she grows "more faithless."

After making love, she and Nick huddle together. This gives her the illusion of safety, though she realizes that it's one of the most dangerous places she could be. She wonders, "How can I assume I know him ... or what he really does?," and jealously fears that the former Handmaid had been there as well. She tells Nick her real name, but he talks little, asks few questions, and appears indifferent, "alive only to the possibilities of my body." Feeling such gratitude toward him, she finds it impossible to imagine betrayal, and she notes that neither of them mentions "love."

She later walks past flower gardens with Ofglen, who encourages her to spy on the Commander; however, Offred is no longer interested. Instead, she heeds Nick's advice not to change anything. (One night, she told Nick that she thinks she's pregnant, though she knows this is "wishful thinking.") She tells Ofglen, not even feigning regret, that she's too afraid to spy on the Commander, but Ofglen says "we" can get people out, if they're in immediate danger. However, Offred doesn't want to escape anymore; she has Nick. She has made a life for herself, she thinks, and this reminds her of something her mother said: "Truly amazing, what people can get used to, as long as there are a few compensations." She notices that Ofglen is giving up on her, whispering less, and talking more about the weather, and Offred feels relief.

In **Chapter 42**, a bell tolls to summon Handmaids, who come without breakfast, and who walk in pairs to witness a women's Salvaging on the old campus library's lawn. Like the Prayvaganza, the women are divided into sections: Wives and daughters, Marthas and Econowives, and Handmaids—in the center so everyone can keep an eye on them, kneeling on small, red velvet cushions. Offred tries to dissociate herself and think about "making love, in the dark," but on the ground in front of her, snaking around and across each row of women, there is a rope that leads to the stage, where two Handmaids and one Wife will be salvaged. Soon, Aunt Lydia and two black-robed Salvagers approach the stage, and Offred shivers with hatred.

Offred tunes out while Aunt Lydia drones on about duty, and spouts platitudes and slogans, but Offred listens when she announces that the reading of the prisoners' crimes will not occur, as there is often a rash of similar crimes when they've been revealed in the past, and the news sends a murmur of disappointment throughout the crowd. Offred explains that the announcement of crimes showed women what they are capable of, but now, they are left guessing, and although she wonders about the Handmaids, she's particularly curious about the Wife: murdering a handmaid? Adultery? Attempted escape?

A Handmaid is the first to be called forward: Ofcharles, who "walks as if she's really concentrating on it," and with an off-center smile on her mouth, she winks at the television camera (though Offred notes that this will be edited out). The Salvagers tie Ofcharles' hands behind her back, put a white bag on her head, help her up onto a stool, then kick it away. Offred, with the rest of the assembled, reaches forward and grabs the rope, then places her hand on her heart to show "my unity with the Salvagers and my consent, and my complicity in the death of this woman."

All three bodies dangle from ropes at the beginning of **Chapter 43**, and Aunt Lydia announces that the Salvaging is concluded, but then, unexpectedly, she instructs the Handmaids to stand and form a circle, which results in some jockeying. Offred knows that she shouldn't hang back too far in such a situation because "it stamps you as lukewarm; lacking in zeal... I don't want to be at the front, or at the back either." Ofglen pulls her up to the second line in the circle, and Offred wonders what will happen next. Aunt Lydia announces that this is a Particicution and tells the Handmaids that what they do after she blows the whistle is up to them, but at the second whistle, they must stop. She signals then, and two Guardians drag a badly beaten man, dressed in a torn, dirty Guardian's uniform, onto the stage. Aunt Lydia announces that the man raped a Handmaid who'd been pregnant, and that the baby died. Offred seethes at this, given what Handmaids must go through, and says that there *is* bloodlust: "I want to tear, gouge, rend." The whistle sounds, and the two Guardians step back from the man, who falls to his knees. At first, everyone hesitates, and Offred tries to look through the man's beaten exterior; she decides he's not Luke, but that he could be Nick: "I know that whatever he's done I can't touch him." The man says, "I didn't ..." but the Handmaids rush him, feeling the adrenaline of freedom, and the first one to reach him is Ofglen: "She pushes him down, sideways, then kicks his head viciously," Offred tells us. Meanwhile, the rest of the Handmaids attack, and Offred is pushed to the ground, only to be helped up by Ofglen, who tells her he wasn't a rapist but "one of ours," and she had put him out of his misery. Aunt Lydia blows her whistle again, but the Handmaids don't stop immediately; the Guardians have to pull them off "from what's left," and many Handmaids have fainted or are injured themselves. Aunt Lydia instructs them to find their partners and form a line, but then Janine comes toward Offred, a clump of hair in her hand and a smile: "her eyes have come loose." Offred understands that she's "let go," but instead of feeling sorry for her, she feels angry. It's an "easy out."

In **Chapter 44**, Offred—after reveling and savoring her lunch, despite its mundane contents—leaves to go shopping, noting that there's "a certain consolation to be taken from routine." She walks out the back door, past Nick, who has his hat on sideways; they avoid looking at each other, afraid that they may give their relationship away. She waits at the corner for Ofglen, who is unusually late, and when she finally arrives, Offred notices that a new Handmaid has taken her old partner's place. The two formally greet each other, and Offred knows that she must play the guessing game all over again: "Is she waiting for me to start something, reveal myself, or is she a believer, engrossed in inner meditation?" Though Offred had just seen Ofglen that morning, and knows Ofglen would have mentioned her transfer if it was coming, Offred asks if a transfer has occurred, to which the new woman simply replies: "I am Ofglen." In an attempt to gauge her new companion, she suggests that they walk to the Wall, where the three women from the morning's Salvaging hang. The new Ofglen says, "Let that be a reminder to us," and Offred tries to discern whether this statement refers to "the unjustness and brutality of the regime," or whether she means that "we should remember to do what we are told and not get into trouble, because if we do we will be rightfully punished." If the latter was Ofglen's intent, Offred should respond by saying, "Praise be," but she decides to take a risk and say "Yes." Ofglen doesn't respond, though she takes a quick look at Offred, and then they begin the long walk home. Offred knows she should not yet push any further, but after they pass the final checkpoint, and there are only blocks to go, Offred can't control herself. In reference to the old

Ofglen, Offred says they met around the first of May, or "May Day," and the new Ofglen says that Offred should forget about such terms from the past; Offred takes this to mean that she's being warned. Offred spends the last part of the walk feeling terrified and stupid; she considers that if the old Ofglen has been captured, she'll mention Offred, and she worries that the authorities will use Luke and her daughter to make her say whatever they want: "I'll incriminate anyone... I'll confess to any crime, I'll end up hanging from a hook on the Wall." However, when she and Ofglen voice the formal farewell at the corner, the new Ofglen leans forward. "She hanged herself," she says, in reference to the former Ofglen. "After the Salvaging. She saw the van coming for her. It was better."

Chapter 45 begins with Offred feeling relieved and thankful that Ofglen killed herself before the authorities arrived: "She has died that I may live," thinks Offred, though she also considers the unsettling possibility that the new Ofglen is lying. Offred comes through the gate and sees Nick washing the car, and she promises God that she'll "empty" herself—give up Nick, forget the others, stop complaining, sacrifice, repent, abdicate, and renounce—but even as she thinks this, she knows she won't do these things; she wants to "keep on living, in any form." She has given in, finally, to the regime. She walks along the garden, toward the back door, when Serena Joy comes out the front door and calls her over. The Wife's angry, and Offred looks at the ground while Serena Joy says, "I trusted you... I tried to help you." Offred can't decide which of her infractions has been discovered, so she stays silent. Fuming, Serena Joy shows her the blue cloak Offred wore to Jezebel's. Serena Joy says there's lipstick on it, drops it, and the feather-and-sequins costume is in her hand; she tosses this to the ground as well. "You could have left me something," Serena Joy says to Offred. She tells her to pick up the costume and go to her room, and says that she's just like the previous Handmaid: "A slut. You'll end the same." Offred stoops to gather the clothes, and she hears that Nick has stopped whistling. She wishes she could turn and run to him, but instead goes into the kitchen through the back door, then heads upstairs.

XV Night

In **Chapter 46**, Offred is waiting, and as the daylight ebbs, she thinks of her options: she could burn the house down; or try to escape; or plead with the Commander; or hang herself; or attack and kill Serena Joy; or simply walk out of the house to see how far she'd get; or go to Nick's room. She then imagines her predecessor "turning in midair under the chandelier, in her costume of stars and feathers," and Offred seems to hear her say, "I'm tired of this melodrama ... There's no one you can protect, your life has value to no one. I want it finished." But as she stands, Offred hears, then sees, the black van in the driveway, from which two men emerge, climb the front steps, and ring the bell. Offred feels angry at herself for not killing herself before; she hears footsteps on the stairs, but she's shocked when Nick throws open the door. She wonders if he's duped her, but he says: "It's Mayday. Go with them," and uses her real name. He disappears, though, when the Eyes escort her down the stairs, past the Commander and Serena Joy, who had clearly been fighting about her. Offred, remarkably, finds she can still feel sorry for the Commander. Serena Joy asks the Eyes what Offred has done—obviously, she hadn't made the call—and the Commander asks for authorization and a warrant. Offred considers screaming and clinging to the banister, thinking that if the Eyes are real, they'll stay, while if they're not, they'll run, but she does nothing. Critics note that in this final set of events, Offred, having lost all agency, let outside events decide her fate—and ironically, she is being let out of Gilead, though not by her own strength. The Eyes say Offred is being arrested for violation of state secrets, and the Commander blanches: "What have I been saying, and to whom, and which one of his enemies has found out?" Serena Joy calls Offred a bitch, saying, "After all he did for you," and the Marthas appear from the kitchen. Cora cries as the Eyes lead Offred from the house to the van. "Whether this is my end or a new beginning I have no way of knowing," Offred says, leaving readers in the same state of suspense.

Historical Notes
on The Handmaid's Tale

This final chapter—the section Atwood scholars discuss and argue about most vehemently—is presented as a transcript from the "Twelfth Symposium on Gileadean Studies," held on June 25, 2195. In it, Atwood appears troubled by why and how our histories are determined, given the removed, arrogant tone of the proceedings, as well as the scholars' manipulation of Offred's manuscript (which readers soon learn about.) But there is good news: because the context for this program is a historical society's convention, Atwood immediately implies the ultimate failure of Gilead's design and empire.

Professor Maryann Crescent Moon—significantly, a *woman*, with a Native American name, linked to the University of Denay, Nunavit—welcomes the conference's participants and credits their interest in this period, since it was responsible for "redrawing the map of the world." Before the keynote speaker begins, however, Professor Crescent Moon makes seemingly pithy announcements that hint at the state of this future world. Upcoming activities at the conference appear to include a fishing expedition, a nature walk, and an Outdoor Period-Costume Sing-Song; the latter event establishes the uncomfortable mawkishness of the gathering, making light of a time during which the worst sorts of crime against humanity were committed.

Also significant are Atwood's name choices, for regarding other announcements, Crescent Moon mentions Professor Johnny Running Dog, Professor Gopal Chatterjee, and Professor Sieglinda Van Buren (of the "Republic of Texas"), as well as Professor James Darcy Pieixoto. The population represented consists of an Indian, two Native Americans, and two people of, most likely, hybridized ethnicity. This being true, it appears that the Gilead regime's anxiety regarding the perpetuation and "survival" of the Caucasian race was well-founded, but the participants' names also indicate that the system, most likely, failed to work.

Crescent Moon introduces Pieixoto, stating that regarding Offred's account, he was "instrumental in its transcription, annotation, and publication," and his talk is titled: "Problems of Authentication in Reference to *The Handmaid's Tale*." Of course, Atwood seems to question the compunction, or *need*, for this text's authentication, suggesting that because the account is that of a woman, the scholars can't, and won't, simply accept the testimonial at face value. And although such an assumption seems cynical, it appears wholly earned when Pieixoto proceeds to make a string of sexual, often misogynist, puns and jokes throughout his talk, including an allusion to "enjoying" a chair in the sexual, "biblical" sense. In addition to the jokes, the audience's laughing acceptance and encouragement indicates that though Gilead, as a system, failed, its seeds—namely reductive misogyny—still remain firmly rooted, acceptable even at the highest levels of thought and education.

Pieixoto credits Professor Knotley Wade with the title *A Handmaid's Tale*, "in homage to the great Geoffrey Chaucer," a *male* literary figure, of course, who has no link to Offred's time or situation, and although this alone could arguably circumscribe Offred's account within a controlling male perspective, there is much more to support this idea. For one thing, we learn that these two men collaborated in order to "construct" Offred's account into a readable manuscript, for "what we have before us is not the item in its original form." According to Pieixoto, the original artifacts were unearthed in Bangor, Maine, "a prominent way station on what our author refers to as 'The Underground Femaleroad,' since dubbed by some of our historical wags 'The Underground Frailroad.' (*Laughter, groans.*)." (Once again, the "joke," and the response, reinforces the idea that women are still not even close to being considered equals.) An old army foot locker, sealed with packing tape, contained thirty cassette tapes onto which Offred recorded her story, and Wade and Pieixoto assumed the task of "transcription."

Each tape, he explains, begins with a few songs of recorded music—no doubt camouflage, he guesses—and then a woman's voice "takes over." The labels on the tapes were authentic, Pieixoto declares, but they didn't always correspond to the recorded music, and the tapes were arranged "in no particular order, being loose at the bottom of the locker; nor were they numbered." This being the case, Wade and Pieixoto took it upon themselves to "arrange the blocks of speech in the order in which they appeared to go... all such arrangements are based on guesswork and are to be regarded as approximate." Of course, Offred's accent, her occasionally obscure references, and "archaisms" made the job even more challenging, and they struggled to define the "nature of the material." To this end, they considered the possibility that it was a forgery, an enterprise that's a direct result of publishers cashing in on the "hypocritical self-congratulation" that often follows a sensationalist account from a "not especially edifying" part of history. But Pieixoto voices a telling aside at this point, cautioning his listeners not to pass moral judgment on the Gileadeans: "Surely we have learned by now that such judgments are culture-specific. Also, Gileadean society was under a good deal of pressure, demographic and otherwise, and was subject to factors from which we ourselves are happily more free. Our job is not to censure but to understand. (*Applause.*)" Not only is this aside self-congratulatory and self-righteous—the very traits he appears to disdain at the outset—but it places Pieixoto in the position of apologist for Gilead's system, which, having read Offred's account, the reader would likely find hard to stomach. The professor's moral relativism, and the audience's apparent support of it, seems to reveal Atwood's skepticism regarding political correctness, particularly its firm grounding in the world of academia.

Pieixoto next argues that Offred successfully escaped, since she must have recorded her account after leaving the Commander's house. For "if the author is telling the truth," Pieixoto pointedly notes, hinting again at a presumption of deceit, "no machine or tapes would have been available to her, nor would she have a place of concealment for them." So, proceeding on the assumption that the tapes were legitimate, he and Wade sought out the identity of the narrator, which proves impossible since hard details are scarce in the account and not much has survived from Gilead itself.

Pieixoto explains that he and Wade held out no hope for tracing the narrator directly, since her name remains forever unknown, and he describes how she landed in her position: Gilead created an "instant pool" of women such as Offred, who were in second marriages or nonmarital liaisons, arresting the women and taking their children for families in the upper class who couldn't conceive.

The reasons for the zero population growth that caused this panic, however, are still sketchy, according to Pieixoto, but it appears to have been a combination of reproductive choices, disease, and, perhaps most importantly, environmental carelessness (toxic waste disposal, biological warfare stockpiles, insecticides, herbicides, etc.). Ironically, of course, the source of these chemicals stem from projects that are intended to protect us, but Atwood appears to warn us that we will do ourselves more harm through these means than any foreign enemy, or bug, would ever do.

Pieixoto next tries to present what can be known about Offred: "Not very much." He quips, "She appears to have been an educated woman, insofar as a graduate of any North American college of the time may be said to have been educated. (*Laughter, some groans.*)" Here, he belittles Offred's intelligence, as well as (again) committing the very "self-congratulation" he eschewed previously. He complains because she "does not see fit" to provide her real name—though this is likely an act of self-protection rather than an affront to future scholars—and notes that the other names provided (Nick, Moira, Janine, Luke) "drew blanks." He posits that these were all pseudonyms, used in order to protect these individuals, and suggests that this indicates that the tapes may have been recorded *within* the bounds of Gilead.

Pieixoto and Wade finally decide that the Commander might be their best hope regarding authentication; based, in part, on the diary of a sociobiologist named Wilfred Limpkin, they decide that the Commander is probably either Frederick R. Waterford or B. Frederick Judd (though, interestingly, there's no speculation about the diarist himself). Frederick Waterford, Pieixoto notes, had a background in marketing and designed the Handmaids' costumes. He may have also invented the Particicution and Salvaging rituals, though, as Pieixoto points out, these were derived from, and synthesized with, practices from earlier histories. On the other hand, historians suspect that B. Frederick Judd of being the mastermind behind the President's Day Massacre, which led to the suspension of the Constitution.

According to Pieixoto, Judd was also of the opinion that the best way to control women was through other women: that is, the Aunts: "When power is scarce, a little of it is tempting." Although the theoretical basis for the Aunts came from Judd, the implementation of the system gets credited to Waterford:

> Who else ... would have come up with the notion that the Aunts should take names derived from commercial products available to women in the immediate pre-Gilead period, and thus familiar and reassuring to them—the names of cosmetic lines, cake mixes, frozen desserts, and even medicinal remedies?

Pieixoto calls this a "brilliant stroke," and posits that this shows Waterford's ingenuity; however, Atwood's readers, by this point, know that the Handmaids were anything but reassured or comforted. This being true, it appears that Atwood wants to alert her readers to how scholars have the power to re-shape and warp the historical record; just as Offred's narrative was questionable regarding reliability, so is Pieixoto's (and any academic's, for that matter), since all information is being processed through a subjective lens.

Pieixoto reports that neither Judd nor Waterford had been married to a Serena Joy (or a Pam) and speculates that Offred used a "malicious" pseudonym here as well; Waterford's wife Thelma, however, did in fact appear on television in pre-Gilead times, in a manner similar to what Offred describes. Thus the evidence, when added up, seems to point to Waterford, who was killed in one of the first purges, soon after the events portrayed in Offred's story. Having been accused of "liberal tendencies, being in possession of a substantial and unauthorized collection of heretical pictorial and literary materials, and of harboring a subversive" (which could have been Offred or Nick), his trial was televised, and Pieixoto notes: "The shots of Waterford are not good, but they are clear enough to establish that his hair was indeed gray."

At this point, Pieixoto reminds his audience that he and his colleague have often had to speculate, and that in spite of their best efforts, there are still many gaps:

> Some of them could have been filled by our anonymous author, had she had a different turn of mind. She could have told us much about the workings of the Gileadean empire, had she had the instincts of a reporter or spy. What would we not give, now, for even twenty pages or so of print-out from Waterford's private computer!

Here, once again, Atwood clearly intends to demonstrate how male narratives are still, in spite of all progress toward gender equality, valued over female narratives. Indeed, Pieixoto follows up his cry with a half-hearted, reconciliatory declaration, saying that historians must be grateful for any "crumbs"—a less than complimentary word choice, given Offred's feat.

Finally, Pieixoto states, "As for the ultimate fate of our narrator, it remains obscure." She may have been recaptured, or she may have escaped to Canada, then to England. If she *did* successfully escape, however, she may have remained silent, for fear of reprisal against her daughter and Luke (though Luke, says Pieixoto, was in all probability dead); or, having difficulty adjusting to life out in the world, she may have become a recluse. Next, the scholars tried to ascertain Nick's motivations for engineering Offred's escape; he knew she would be interrogated if caught, and though he could have perhaps protected himself most by assassinating her, Pieixoto notes, "the human heart remains a factor, and, as we know, both of them thought she might be pregnant by him." Ultimately, of course, this escape plan may have been Nick's downfall.

Pieixoto condescends to the manuscript one last time, patronizingly calling it "in its own way eloquent," and then refs to the elusive quality of such subjects of study: "when we turn to look at her we glimpse her only for a moment, before she slips from our grasp and flees." Though Offred appears to have escaped, she does not, in the end, seem to succeed in wholly re-creating herself through language; in fact, she exists forever as she has as a Handmaid, when people could only look at and see her in short flashes of time. Pieixoto closes his speech by saying that we can't always decipher voices from the past "in the clearer light of our own day." However, this leaves the reader with the impression that Pieixoto is making things harder than they have to be by viewing Offred's account as "imbued with ... obscurity" rather than as an important testimonial—history turned "her-story," which he seems to suspect, if not outright reject. Atwood certainly seems to imply, in this final section, that we must be both cognizant about *who* writes/determines our history and skeptical about the motivations, prejudices, and ideology that inform such interpretation. Even though Offred dedicated a lot of effort to construct a record, as well as herself, she is ultimately re-constructed and defined by male academics, making them, in a sense, the present-day Commanders of our past.

Critical Views

MARGARET ATWOOD ON THE CREATION
OF *THE HANDMAID'S TALE**

Some critics have called the novel a feminist tract. "Novels are not slogans," Miss Atwood responds. "If I wanted to say just one thing I would hire a billboard. If I wanted to say just one thing to one person, I would write a letter. Novels are something else. They aren't just political messages. I'm sure we all know this, but when it's a book like this you have to keep on saying it. The book is an examination of character under certain circumstances, among other things. It's not a matter of men against women. That happens to be in the book because I think if it were going to happen in the United States, that's the form it would take. But it's a study of power, and how it operates and how it deforms or shapes the people who are living within that kind of regime.

"You could say it's a response to 'it can't happen here.' When they say 'it can't happen here,' what they usually mean is Iran can't happen here, Czechoslovakia can't happen here. And they're right, because this isn't there. But what could happen here? It wouldn't be some people saying, 'Hi, folks, we're Communists and we're going to be your new Government.' But if you were going to do it, what would you do? What emotions would you appeal to? What groups would you utilize? How exactly would you go about it? Well, something like the way the religious right is doing things. And the ultimate result of that process would be the union of church and state, which this country since 1776 has striven to keep apart, with great difficulty, because the foundation of this country was not separation of church and state. We're often taught in schools that the Puritans came to America for religious freedom. Nonsense. They came to establish their own regime, where they could persecute people to their heart's content just the way they themselves had been persecuted. If

77

you think you have the word and the right way, that's the only thing you can do."

* Interview conducted by Mervyn Rothstein for the *New York Times*.

BARBARA EHRENREICH
ON FEMINIST DYSTOPIA

The feminist imagination has been far more productive of utopias (from Charlotte Perkins Gilman's *Herland* to Marge Piercy's *Woman on the Edge of Time*) than of dystopias, and for good reason. Almost every thinkable insult to women has been tested and institutionalized at one time or another: foot-binding, witch-burning, slavery, organized rape, ritual mutilation, enforced childbearing, enforced chastity, and the mere denial of ordinary rights to own property, speak out in public, or walk down a street without fear. For misogynist nastiness, it is hard to improve on history.

Yet there has been no shortage of paranoid folklore about what the future may hold for women. Since the early 1970s, one important strand of feminist thought (usually called "cultural" or radical" feminist) has tended to see all of history as a male assault on women and, by proxy, on nature itself. Hence rape, hence acid rain, hence six-inch high heels, hence the arms race, hence (obviously) the scourge of pornography. Extrapolating from this miserable record, cultural feminists have foreseen women being driven back to servitude as breeders and scullery maids, or else, when reproductive technology is refined enough to make wombs unnecessary, being eliminated altogether. The alternative, they believe, is to create a "women's culture," envisioned as intrinsically loving, nurturing, and in harmony with nature—before we are all destroyed by the toxic effects of testosterone.

Margaret Atwood's new novel is being greeted as the long-awaited feminist dystonia and I am afraid that for some time it will be viewed as a test of the imaginative power of feminist paranoia. (...)

But if Offred is a sappy stand-in for Winston Smith, and Gilead seems at times to be only a coloring book version of Oceania, it may be because Atwood means to do more than scare us about the obvious consequences of a Falwellian coup d'état. There is a subtler argument at work in *The Handmaid's Tale*, and it is as intellectually interesting as the fictional world she has housed it in. We are being warned, in this tale, not only about the theocratic ambitions of the religious right, but about a repressive tendency in feminism itself. Only on the surface is Gilead a fortress of patriarchy, Old Testament style. It is also, in a thoroughly sinister and distorted way, the utopia of cultural feminism.

There is, for example, no pornography in the new world (even the Bible is kept under lock and key); there are no cosmetics or other artifices to insult the natural female form, and the punishment for rape is to be torn to bits by a mob of women. Men, including physicians, have been barred from the scene of childbirth, which is now assisted by a ritual circle of chanting handmaids. In the Red Center where handmaids are trained for service, the presiding "Aunts" indoctrinate their charges in a twisted proto-feminist ideology: women were once subject to hideous abuse by men, but now they are "free" from all that, while men have been reduced, for all practical purposes, to stud service. Aunt Lydia even offers oblique praise for the more separatist feminists of our own time, and dreams of a future in which "Women will live in harmony with each other ... Women united for a common end!" The irony is not lost on Offred, whose own mother had been something of a feminist termagant, fond of pornographic book burnings. "You wanted a women's culture," Offred thinks, addressing her mother. "Well, now there is one. It isn't what you meant, but it exists."

Revolutionaries seldom do get exactly what they want, but at least with *The Handmaid's Tale* we stand warned. There has been an ominous convergence between some of the ideas of the antifeminist right and those of the cultural feminist militants. The antifeminists would like to get us all back to the kitchen, but they are also responsible for some of the most strident female supremacist literature to come out of the last two decades' gender wars. (See, for example, Phyllis Schlafly's *The Power of the Positive Woman*.) The cultural feminists, for their part, would like women to be free agents in the public sphere, but other feminists argue that their views on sex may be ultimately repressive to women. On the issue of pornography, the two sides appear to agree wholeheartedly, although just what it is, and whether it might even be defined to include a thoroughly feminist nightmare like *The Handmaid's Tale*, no one can say.

This tale is an absorbing novel, as well as an intra-feminist polemic. Still, it does remind us that, century after century, women have been complicit in their own undoing. Like the sadistic Aunts in *The Handmaid's Tale*, it was women who bound their granddaughters' feet, women who turned over their little girls for clitoridectomies, and often even women who denounced their neighbors as witches.

CATHARINE R. STIMPSON
ON "ATWOOD WOMAN"

The central figure in Atwood's territory is a woman. Atwood Woman is young, educated, white, middle class, invariably heterosexual. She has a job—as an illustrator, scientist, journalist. She has had her share of sexual experience. Her men are often weaker than she. She is urban, but the wilderness is usually the site of her most profound moral and psychological education. In flight from her day-to-day life, she discovers the meaning of survival, a key word in Atwood's vocabulary. She is Marian in Atwood's comedy of manners, *The Edible Woman*; the nameless narrator in the quest novel, *Surfacing*; Joan, the Gothic fraud, in that wonderful romp, *Lady Oracle*; Lesje and Elizabeth in the somber chamber piece, *Life Before Man*; Rennie in a second quest novel, set in the Caribbean rather than in Canada, *Bodily Harm*. Now she is Offred.

Flanking Atwood Woman are two other sorts of women, both of whom influence her. One is her contemporary, often more raucous or audacious than she. The second sort of woman is older. She is Atwood Woman's landlady, employer, aunt, mother, neighbor. Reactionary and manipulative, she strips the world of sensuality and spontaneity. Terrified of the naked, she nevertheless denudes her environment. Her ideals are decency, respectability. Acting on them, she commits moral indecency after moral indecency. She enjoys watching the wormings and turnings of another's submission. Frequently these toughies, in their hats, gloves and woolen underwear, represent provincial Anglo-Canadian society. In *Bodily Harm*, Rennie says sardonically of Griswold, Ontario, her hometown: "In Griswold everyone gets what they deserve. In Griswold everyone deserves the worst."

Gilead is Griswold gone wild. The Aunts, who pump iron (but never irony) into the body politic of technological Calvinism, represent Atwood's most disdainful depiction of the petty female boss. Wearing electric cattle prods on leather belts, they control, reward and punish other women. Like certain of Brecht's characters, they are at once sinister and funny. Atwood achieves a triple effect—she makes her dystopic state even more frightening because it issues cattle prods to such ordinary figures. Yet she also manages to domesticate totalitarianism, because she shows it peopled by such ordinary figures. The state becomes even more frightening, because its monstrosity seems normally absurd, absurdly normal. Finally, Atwood reminds her reader of the political function of satire: to weaken the grip of the cruel and foolish by sending them up witless.

In one of her most original maneuvers, Atwood links the morality of the Aunts to that of radical feminists. The Aunts are repressive. Radical feminists can be repressive too. In the active syllogism of power, the premises of repression lead to conclusions of oppression.

AMIN MALAK ON ATWOOD
IN THE DYSTOPIAN TRADITION

The state in Gilead prescribes a pattern of life based on frugality, conformity, censorship, corruption, fear, and terror—in short, the usual terms of existence enforced by totalitarian states, instance of which can be found in such dystopian works as Zamyatin's *We*, Huxley's *Brave New World*, and Orwell's *1984*.

In order to situate Atwood's novel within the relevant context of dystopia, I wish to articulate the salient dystopian features those three classics reveal. The ensuing discussion will be an elaboration on Atwood's rendition and redefinition of those features.

1. Power, Totalitarianism, War:

Dystopias essentially deal with power: power as the prohibition or perversion of human potential; power in its absolute form that, to quote from *1984*, tolerates no flaws in the pattern it imposes on society. Dystopias thus show, in extreme terms, power functioning efficiently and mercilessly to its optimal totalitarian limit. Interestingly, war or foreign threats often loom in the background, providing the pretext to join external tension with internal terror.

2. Dream-Nightmare: Fantasy: Reality:

While dystopias may be fear-laden horror fiction (how the dream turns into a nightmare), the emphasis of the work is not on horror for its own sake, but on forewarning. Similarly, while dystopias contain elements of the fantastic with a "touch of excess" carrying the narrative "one step [or more] beyond our reality,"[2] the aim is neither to distort reality beyond recognition, nor to provide an escapist world for the reader, but "to allow certain tendencies in modern society to spin forward without the brake of sentiment and humaneness."[3]

3. Binary Oppositions:

Dystopias dramatize the eternal conflict between individual choice and social necessity: the individual resenting the replacement of his private volition by compulsory uniformitarian decisions made by an impersonal bureaucratic machinery; Zamyatin's heroine poignantly sums up the conflict: "I do not want anyone to want for me. I want to want for myself."[4] The sphere of the binary opposition expands further to cover such dialectical dualities as emotion and reason, creative imagination and mathematical logic, intuition and science, tolerance and judgment, kindness and cruelty, spirituality and materialism, love and power, good and evil. The list can go on.

4. Characterization:

Dystopias often tend to offer two-dimensional character types; this tendency is possibly due to the pressure of the metaphorical and ideological thrust of these works. Moreover, the nightmarish atmosphere of dystopias seems to preclude advancing positive, assertive characters that might provide the reader with consoling hope. If such positive characters do exist, they usually prove miserably ineffectual when contending with ruthless overwhelming powers.

5. Change and Time:

Dystopian societies, consumed and controlled by regressive dogmas, appear constantly static: founded on coercion and rigid structures, the system resists change and becomes arrested in paralysis. Such a static life "shorn of dynamic possibility," becomes for the underprivileged members of society mediocre, monotonous and predictable: "a given and measured quantity that can neither rise to tragedy nor tumble to comedy."[5]

Accordingly, dystopias are not associated with innovation and progress, but with fear of the future. They use, however, the present as an instructive referent, offering a tacit alternative to the dystopian configuration.

6. Roman à These:

To varying degrees, dystopias are quintessentially ideological novels: they engage the reader in what Fredrick Jameson calls a "theoretical discourse," whereby a range of thematic possibilities are posited and polarized against each other, yet the novels eventually reveal a definite philosophical and socio-political outlook for which fiction proves to be a convenient medium.

What distinguishes Atwood's novel form those dystopian classics is its obvious feminist focus. (...)

While the major dystopian features can clearly be located in *The Handmaid's Tale*, the novel offers two distinct additional features: feminism and irony. Dramatizing the interrelationship between power and sex, the book's feminism, despite condemning male misogynous mentality, upholds and cherishes a man-woman axis; here, feminism functions inclusively rather than exclusively, poignantly rather than stridently, humanely rather than cynically. The novel's ironic tone, on the other hand, betokens a confident narrative strategy that aims at treating a depressing material gently and gradually, yet firmly, openly, and conclusively, thus skilfully succeeding in securing the reader's sympathy and interest. The novel shows Atwood's strengths both as an engaging story-teller and a creator of a sympathetic heroine, and as an articulate crafts-woman of a theme that is both current and controversial. As the novel signifies a landmark in the maturing process of Atwood's creative career, her self-assured depiction of the grim dystopian world gives an energetic and meaningful impetus to the genre.

Notes
2. Irving Howe in *1984 Revisited: Totalitarianism in Our Century*, ed. Irving Howe (New York: Harper and Row, 1983), p. 8.
3. Irving Howe, *Politics and the Novel* (New York: Horizon Press, 1957), p. 242.
4. Yevgeny Zamyatin, *We*, trans. Mirra Ginsberg (New York: Viking, 1972), p. v.
5. *Politics and the Novel*, p. 240.

ARNOLD E. DAVIDSON
ON "HISTORICAL NOTES"

Yet Offred's perturbing narration does not comprise the whole of *The Handmaid's Tale*. Appended to the fifteen titled sections that constitute her account and the bulk of the novel is a final part not numbered as another section nor even designated as a separate chapter. These "Historical Notes" give us both a second future (a future to Gilead) and the genealogy of Offred's account, which up to that point we have been reading. The resultant disjunction might well seem disconcerting. After an appalling story of tyranny, genocide, and gynocide in late twentieth-century America, we are, in effect, brought fast-forward to June 25, 2195, to the University of Denay in Nunavit and an International Historical Association's rather placid (if pompous) intellectual foray back into the Gilead Regime.

This unequal division of the text serves several narrative functions. On a most immediate level, the second part provides, as previously noted, the history of Offred's history and an account of how her private record has become a public document, the object of future historians' attention. That attention, moreover, supplements Offred's story by the very act of subjecting it to academic scrutiny. Whereas Offred describes the practices of Gilead, the Twelfth Symposium on Gileadean Studies can provide some of the theory that underlies those practices. Thus, we are given the analysis of the use of the "Aunts" as especially "cost-effective" or the observation that

Gilead itself was partly the product of earlier theories such as the sociobiology of Wilfred Limpkin. A retrospective symposium attests, too, that Gilead was survived and as such constitutes a distinct note of hope for the future. But that note is countered by another consideration. The historical notes, like any scholarly afterword, also serve to validate the text that they follow, and there is something ominous in that claiming of the right to have the last word.

Retrospective analysis by a Cambridge don—male, of course—is ostensibly more authoritative than a participant woman's eyewitness account. Furthermore, the supposed "objectivity" of the scholarly enterprise of the Twelfth Symposium on Gileadean Studies is a chilling postscript to a story in which women (and others too: blacks, Jews, homosexuals, Quakers, Baptists) have been totally *objectified*, rendered into objects by the State. Is the process beginning again? And implicit in that question is a more immediate one. Do we, as scholars, contribute to the dehumanizations of society by our own critical work, especially when, as according to the distinguished professor of the novel, "our job is not to censure but to understand"?[1] Atwood's epilogue loops back through the text that precedes it to suggest that the ways in which scholars (present as well as future) assemble the text of the past confirms the present and thereby helps to predict the future, even the horrific future endured by Offred. In short, Atwood does not let intellectuals off the hook—and the hook is a loaded metaphor in *The Handmaid's Tale*. How we *choose* to construct history partly determines the history we are likely to get.

Another version of this same problematic of history is implicit in the textual question posed by the epilogue: "The Handmaid's Tale" in its present form is not the only possible ordering of the "some thirty tapes" (we are never told exactly how many) that have been transcribed (we are never told how directly) into text. The editors, we are specifically informed, have intervened to make choices about the structure of the tale. Moreover, Professor Knotly Wade of Cambridge and Professor James Darcy Pieixoto, Director of the Twentieth and Twenty-

First Century Archives at Cambridge, have ordered thirty or so tapes into an extremely intricate structure—forty-six untitled chapters arranged in fifteen labeled sections, with the heading "Night" used seven times (and the only heading repeated). Professor Pieixoto admits that "all such arrangements are based on some guesswork and are to be regarded as approximate, pending further research". But that pro forma disclaimer does not acknowledge how much the very process of assembling a text (or writing the history of any age from its surviving traces) means *creating* a fiction. Where, then, is the boundary between novel and history? This textual question becomes all the more pertinent when juxtaposed against Atwood's insistence that everything in the book is "true," has, in some form in some society, already been done (Cathy N. Davidson, "A Feminist *1984*"). (...)

The historical notes with which *The Handmaid's Tale* ends provide comic relief from the grotesque text of Gilead. Yet in crucial ways the epilogue is the most pessimistic part of the book. Even with the lesson Gilead readily at hand, the intellectuals of 2195 seem to be preparing the way for Gilead again. In this projection of past, present, and future, the academic community is shown to have a role, not simply an "academic" role (passive, accommodating) but an active one in recreating the values of the past—which is, Atwood suggests, the way to create the values of the future. Professor Pieixoto's title is "Problems of Authentication in Reference to *The Handmaid's Tale*," and his very mode of speaking authenticates her tale by retrospectively duplicating the suppression her society inflicted upon her, by claiming the right to determine the meaning of her experience. But because his reading of her experience verges back towards Gilead again, our reading of his reading can authenticate Offred's account in a different sense than the professor intended and can also show how insidious are the horrors at the heart of his dark narrative.

The professor, too, concludes with mixed metaphors of light and dark: "As all historians know, the past is a great darkness, and filled with echoes. Voices may reach us from it; but what they say to us is imbued with the obscurity of the matrix out of which they come; and, try as we may, we cannot always decipher them precisely in the clearer light of our own day". It is a brief peroration that elicits his audience's applause and prepares the way for any discussion that might follow. Indeed, when he ends, with again a standard ploy—"Are there any questions?"—that question itself well may be rhetorical. And even if it is not, the speaker has already indicated what he thinks the questions are. His questions, however, need not be our questions, especially when we consider the matrix out of which his asking comes. His persistent assertion of gender prerogatives darkens his claimed "clearer light of [his] own day" and conjoins his world with Gilead's and ours.

Note

1. Atwood, *The Handmaid's Tale* (Toronto: McClelland and Stewart, 1985), p. 315. Page references in this text are to this edition.

MARTA CAMINERO-SANTANGELO ON RESISTENT POSTMODERNISM

A recognition of complicity with mass culture, along with an understanding that only within this arena can effective resistance be waged, marks *The Handmaid's Tale* as what Huyssen might call a resistant postmodern novel. The text presents itself as a hybrid of two highly popular fictional forms, science fiction and the woman's romance. The latter elements have drawn much negative criticism from feminist critics who ask, along with Sandra Tomc, "Why ... does Atwood choose to resolve her drama of women's oppression by implementing a paradigm of the female romance, such that the telos of the heroine's journey becomes her introduction to Mr Right?" (73). Tomc subsequently answers her own question by drawing upon the conflict between elitist academic discourse and popular culture:

> The 'Historical Notes' indicate that a tribute to the 'low brow,' to forms of culture inadmissible to scholarly exchange, is part of her project. It is no accident that Offred's tapes are discovered among other tokens of popular passion and bad taste—Elvis Presley tunes, folk songs, Mantovani instrumentals, and the screams of Twisted Sister—nor that all of these are laughed at and dismissed by Professor Pieixoto. (82)

What is at stake, however, is more than just an arbitrary "tribute" to low culture. It is the postmodern recognition that popular culture is the only field of effective ideological battle.

Within the narrative, media—whether in the Gileadean present of most of the novel or in the handmaid's "past"—are never approached in a purely adversarial relation. Although films, news broadcasts, etc., are presented as tools for ideological indoctrination, popular songs and ladies' magazines "from the time before" (81) have a peculiarly subversive potential in Gilead; and even the news is not rejected outright as misinformation. The narrator (whom I will refer to as "Offred" for lack of a better name) acknowledges the possibility that the footage she is shown is "faked," but she hopes nevertheless to "read beneath it" (105). The mass media are certainly a technology for the production of (the dominant) ideology, but they also hold the potential for a locus of resistance to that ideology. Rejecting the characteristically modernist stance of alienation from institutionalized discourses, the resistant postmodern speaks, and attempts to subvert, from within; though Offred initially refuses to call the room where she sleeps "my room" (11), and thus positions herself outside the Gileadean order, eventually (in the wake of the Commander's invasion of her room) she responds by claiming a space for herself: "My room, then. There has to be some space, finally, that I claim as mine" (66).

In *The Handmaid's Tale* Atwood is caught in the dilemma faced by many creators of satiric dystopias: the author needs both to condemn particular social injustices and to portray the mechanisms of oppression as credible enough, as sufficiently powerful and seductive, to represent a believable evil, not an irrelevant or far-fetched one. While attempting to balance ethical interests with plausibility, the ambitious author risks falling into either transparent didacticism or a contradictory fascination with the rhetorical machinery of dystopic horror. Atwood's discourse in marked by stylistic and rhetorical features—habits of syntactic and lexical arrangement and strategies of managing point of view and addresser-addressee relations—that show she has succumbed to the latter: scenes of violence and horror meant to illuminate sites of oppression are also strategically designed to manipulate and horrify. Atwood's narrator is an authoritative and authoritarian storyteller, one who manipulates the reader as she tells her story but one who is also caught in the web of Gileadan power politics. Offred's powerful narrative skill conflicts with the powerlessness, the innocence, and the descriptive phenomenological cast of mind that also characterize her. It is as if Atwood's skill as storyteller continually intrudes, possessing her narrative creation. Narrative self-consciousness, in fact, does explicitly and strategically emerge. (...)

In *The Handmaid's Tale* the reader is addressed by a narrator whose authority is sanctioned by the implied author: she possesses an analytical intelligence that demonstrates her clear superiority over others. She is a reader of the social "signs" in her environment and in everyday objects. Offred is assigned the authority of an implied author; there is, in fact, no gap between implied author and narrator, no attempt to distinguish the voices. There is, however, a tension between Offred's narrative skill and the characterization of her as a Handmaid. This narrator wants the discourse freedoms and powers normally granted only to men; yet she is in the position of Handmaid:

The pen between my fingers is sensuous, alive almost, I can feel its power, the power of the words it contains. Pen is envy, Aunt Lydia would say, quoting another Centre motto, warning us way from such objects. And they were one more right, it is envy. Just holding it is envy. I envy the Commander his pen. It's one more thing I would like to steal. (196)

The intelligence and wit of the narrator is but one of various rhetorical tactics that Atwood uses to induce our acceptance of the didactic authenticity of her satire. Its social and intellectual validity as argument is enforced by a narrator who shifts between readerly footings of intimacy and equality to footings of authority, superior insight, and impersonal detachment. (...)

What I am trying to suggest is that Atwood's narrator in this novel does not speak entirely in the voice of the victim, the writer who pleads "Mayday"; rather, she speaks in the skilled voice of the rhetorician and the fabulator who is purposefully telling a story. Atwood has the narrator move through her thoughts in a plain style, joining modifying phrases to the main clause on the right side of the sentence, as if to suggest syntactically the artlessness of the narrator. The co-ordinate structures and right-branching sentences, however, are filled with an abstract lexis, a lexis of contemplativeness that emphasizes the narrator's wisdom, her philosophical and emotional superiority over those around her: "We yearned for the future. How did we learn it, that talent for insatiability? I was in the air; and it was still in the air, an afterthought, as we tried to sleep, in the army cots that had been set up in rows, with spaces between so we could not talk." (The rhetorical question here is another indicator of the author's artfullness.) Here we encounter a paradox: the voluble narrator speaks confidently and precisely about the silence she endured. To increase the sense of the macabre sinisterness of the setting, Atwood's narrator plays on the tension between the domestic softness and military harshness, between the cozy flannelette sheets and "Aunts" and the rough "army-issue" blankets and menacing "electric cattle prods slung on thongs."

The Handmaid's Tale, I would argue, quite strongly enforces the handmaid's limited perspective upon the reader. Two devices in particular seem to work towards this end. One is the large number of textual interpellations, in which the handmaid seems to speak for all women/all who would read the text as women. These are statements in the plural "we," statements which have the effect of creating an identification: you, reader, woman, are like me: abject. Interpellations begin on the first page. "We yearned for the future," says the handmaid from the Red Centre. "How did we learn it, that talent for insatiability?" (13). Later she suggests that all the women at the centre recognize their only resource as their bodies. "If only we could talk to [the guards]. Something could be exchanged, we thought, some deal made, some trade-off, we still had our bodies. That was our fantasy" (14). On numerous occasions the handmaid adopts this non-contradictory collective voice, as for instance when she describes the mode of living in the time before the revolution: "We lived, as usual, by ignoring" (66).

The implication is that all women share the characteristics of the handmaid, an impression ironically strengthened by the fact that, in her very namelessness, the handmaid takes on the guise of an Everywoman. The interpellations strengthen the reader's identification with the handmaid. Again, the political intention may be to produce a kind of revulsion: how dare this woman speak for me? But conventional reading practice accords a certain authority to a narrator, even a limited narrator, and there is little within *The Handmaid's Tale* to offer another position. To say, as the handmaid does, that "I resign my body freely" is of course the ultimate ideological effect; but without a sense of alternatives, of contradiction (I give up my body to live, but giving up my body attacks the very reason for me to be alive) the narrative implies that the resignation of her body is somehow "natural" for the handmaid, that the lack of contradiction (which is the very possibility of struggle) is not, in fact, an effect of ideology, but is somehow part of her woman's "being."

The second device is the presentation and devaluation of alternatives. The protagonist's mother, Moira, and Ofglen all seem to represent alternatives to the handmaid's passivity But the "plot" of the novel (with all the conspiratorial resonances) works to delegitimize these alternatives. The handmaid's mother, who has spent her life in feminist struggle, is revealed by the middle of the story to have ended up as a bitter old alcoholic. She only retains her belief that history will absolve her "after the third drink" (131). The mother's sorry end is part of a satire directed against "radical" feminists, who are portrayed in the novel as contributing to the intolerant mentality that leads to Gilead. Moira, perhaps the most dynamic representative of resistance, is shown by the end to have cynically accepted her lot as a prostitute. "I mean, I'm not a martyr," she says. The whorehouse is not so bad: "Butch paradise, you might call it" (261). Ofglen distinguishes herself with two acts of courage: the mercy killing of the "rapist" and her own suicide to protect her comrades. Her courage, however, is devalued by the handmaid's reactions to it. The news of Ofglen's sacrifice does not generate anger or sympathy in the handmaid. Instead she feels "thankful" (298). For the handmaid, Ofglen's courage only highlights the risks of action, and thus contributes to her own abjection. The result, for me as a reader, is to increase my feeling of hopelessness: if Ofglen's sacrifice cannot inspire the least resolve in the handmaid—the Everywoman of *The Handmaid's Tale*—then her sacrifice seems to be without value, to be even, perhaps, an act of madness.

PAMALA COOPER ON VOYERISM AND THE FILMING OF *THE HANDMAID'S TALE*

With the sinister politics of looking explored so pervasively in the novel, the dominant irony in the relation of written text to film seems to be the movie's very existence. To film *The Handmaid's Tale* is to duplicate the threatening strategies of visual surveillance that persecute the women depicted in the narrative. It is to force the audience's complicity by identifying the inherent voyeurism of movie-watching(12) with the invasive examining of the disenfranchised by the dictatorial which the novel portrays. The very act of filming *The Handmaid's Tale* automatically shifts the issue of surveillance-enforced misogyny to a metafictional or metacinematic level. Here the politics of looking operate on a wider social and psychological basis, with explicit reference to the role of the spectator and the mechanization of vision through the agency of the camera. The film, moving beyond the literal scope of the narrative but unable to escape its logic, installs the camera as the ultimately reified eye, the site where vision is perfectly displaced away from the human body and onto the machine. In this way the movie seals and implicitly endorses the terms of that contract, so vehemently questioned in the novel, between totalitarianism and the gaze.

Given the audience's involuntary assumption, through the specularizing apparatus of the camera, of the subject position of spectator,(13) the power of the gaze which accrues to any watcher of movies sits with peculiar unease upon the optics of the viewer of *The Handmaid's Tale*. Physically implicated in the objectifying practices of cinematic looking,(14) such a viewer is equally implicated psychologically—in the objectifying practices of despotic looking thematized in the novel. Co-opted in this way by a combination of filmic form and narrative content, the viewer may experience the movie as a kind of acting out—at least on the level of the film's aesthetic reality—of the political oppression detailed in the text. The immediacy of the visual medium traps the viewer of *The Handmaid's Tale* in an especially piquant double bind, by its radical alteration of the terms of readerly engagement with the written text. Transforming the indirect, more abstract and generalized voyeurism of reading into the physically prompt voyeurism of watching, the movie invites the viewer to the very pleasures of looking reproved by the novel. Activating fully the eroticism of surveillance without the experiential or situational distance available to a reader, the film of *The Handmaid's Tale* reinscribes, through the procedures of another medium, the very terms of fascist authority which the novel critiques. In this respect, the inclusion of the movie in the first post-Cold War film festival in Berlin was almost absurdly ironic.

For the woman viewer, this double bind is particularly painful. Struggling with cinematic conventions which force her to assume the position of gazer while also encoding her as the ultimate object of filmic representation, the female spectator is at once tempted by and excluded from visual pleasure: "In their traditional exhibitionist role women are simultaneously looked at and displayed, with their appearance coded for strong visual and erotic impact so that they can be said to connote to-be-looked-at-ness. Woman displayed as sexual object is the leitmotif of erotic spectacle ... she holds the look, plays to and signifies male desire" (Mulvey, "Visual" 62, emphasis in original). Yet, while her invitation to the delights of spying is paradoxically dependent upon her compromised ability to enjoy them, her situation as spectator, though ambiguous, implicates her in the invasive violence of surveillance. Caught both ways, a woman viewing *The Handmaid's Tale* finds herself in a position of partial and equivocal empowerment, similar in effect to those women in the novel who are co-opted but not fully enfranchised by the system. The Aunts enforce the laws of Gilead and actively oppress other women; to watch this movie as a woman is to become a kind of Aunt—experiencing the anguish of complicity without its compensations.

KAREN STEIN ON FRAME AND DISCOURSE

A key stylistic feature of *Tale* is its use of layers of textual material to establish frames that set up ironic oscillations of meaning. The epigraphs, historical notes and dedications are part of this process, but even within Offred's narrative the novel employs this ironic layering device. First, we note that Offred's text, the main portion of the novel, is Pieixoto's piecing together of recorded fragments. Second, within the tale puns, digressions, flashbacks, asides, rewordings, abound. Offred sometimes retells the same event in different ways, reminding us that this is a "reconstruction" or an "approximation."

Thus, Offred's words continue the pattern of layered texts, overlapping voices within the novel. Jill LeBihan notes that this textual layering functions to problematize the Gileadean notion that there exists one truth, one officially sanctioned version of reality: "the novel constantly reiterates its uncertain, problematic relationship with the concept of a single reality, one identity, a truthful history". Further,

> the dystopian genre and temporal shifts are ways of drawing attention to the frame, the arrangers, and the white space and flat surfaces which make perception ... possible (104) ... *The Handmaid's Tale* is dystopian fiction, but also historiographic metafiction with a confessional journal-style first person narrator. The single identifiable generic frame is stretched to include as many different writing strategies as possible within its construction. But the story once in print ... is not under the subject's control (106).

(...)

The overlapping frames of discourse, the background noises (puns, allusions, digressions, memories, retellings, multiplicity of genres, disconnections); these are among the devices which construct *The Handmaid's Tale*. There are many voices, starting with the dedication, moving through the epigraphs and the journal-entry novel to the Historical Notes. The "crisis of interpretation" is situated within Offred and Pieixoto. To agree with Offred, we must become complicit in the voyeurism of Gilead and its sexual and political violence; we must rectify the romance plot which engineers Offred's escape from Gilead. To agree with Pieixoto, we must acquiesce to moral relativism and patriarchal sexism. "There is no solace or privilege for the critic in all of this": we must interrogate our own readings; in the person of Pieixoto ("analytically adept, logical to a fault, [a] keen student of the literary text") we have already been subsumed into the text. Layers of overlapping texts "rewrite, recycle, and permanently distort one text by [another] ...

version of it." The incursions from the margins, the dedications and epigraphs which pressing upon the text, the Historical Notes which rewrite the tale from a future time add "further and implosive level[s]."

LOIS FEUER ON THE HANDMAID'S TALE AND 1984

Because Orwell's work is the best known in this series, it is to 1984 that *The Handmaid's Tale* has most frequently been compared.

The resemblances are many, and perhaps inescapable given the totalitarian regimes under which both protagonists live. In both, we have the distinctively modern sense of nightmare come true, the initial paralyzed powerlessness of the victim unable to act. Paradoxically, given this mood of waking nightmare, both novels use nighttime dreams and memory flashes to recapture the elusive past through which their protagonists try to retain their individual humanity. But individual humanity is, of course, undesirable in the society-as-prison; as in Kafka's emblematic penal colony, language (books for women in *The Handmaid's Tale*; connotative, reflective speech in *1984*) is restricted and controlled as an instrument of power; in *The Handmaid's Tale*, Harvard itself, bastion of reasoned discourse, has become the site of torture and mutilation of the regime's enemies.

As Oceania both was and was not the postwar London of Orwell's time, Gilead both is and is not the United States we know. Serena Joy, the Commander's wife, bears an ironic resemblance to Phyllis Schlafly, taking a public position that women should not take public positions.[4] This referential topicality exists because both authors envision the future by extrapolating from tendencies in the present; as Blake points out, a prophet is one who tells us that if we keep on doing x, y will be the result. Both novels envision a society in which perpetual war is used as a rationale for internal repression. The ease with which the authorities in *1984* switch the identity of the enemy makes it clear, long before Winston reads Goldstein's confirmatory analysis, that the "enemy" is a pretext; the epilogue to *The Handmaid's Tale* makes explicit the secret agreement between the superpowers that enabled them to concentrate on subjugating their own people (388). Both are societies purged of diversity and individuality, based on sexism, racism, and elitism, in which private relationships between friends and lovers become-or become seen as-subversive acts.[5]

Thus Atwood gives us all the hallmarks of a totalitarian society set forth in 1984 (Hadomi 209–17) and originated by Zamiatin in We: public spectacle as means of control, the two-minute hate and Hate Week, and the Salvaging and Prayvaganza. The fear of spies and betrayal are constants: Handmaids part with the phrase "Under His Eye," just as Oceanians knew that Big Brother was watching. Lack of privacy and constant surveillance are common features; thus the eye is a continuing image in *The Handmaid's Tale*, from the name of the secret police to the symbol tattooed on Offred's ankle.[6] This threat of betrayal-Winston suspects Julia as Offred does Nick-has already begun to destroy Offred's relationship with her husband Luke before he is (presumably) shot while they are trying to escape to Canada (232, 236). Despite this threat, both societies have-or have rumors of-an underground resistance network; at the open-ended conclusion of Atwood's novel, it is ostensibly this network, of which Nick is a member, that enables Offred to escape to the safe house in Maine where she dictates the tapes of which the novel purports to be a transcription.

In both works, loss of identity is an ever-present threat, this submersion of the self represented by color-coded uniforms denoting the status of the wearer, whether Inner or Outer Party member or Commander, Guardian, or Handmaid. The danger is real: Offred at times becomes subsumed by her category and thinks of herself as "we" (203), and Atwood uses the motif of the double throughout the novel to represent this threat. Describing another Handmaid walking away, Offred says, "She's like my own reflection, in a mirror from which I am moving away" (59; also 25, 31, 213). The motif of the double is a continuing one in Atwood's work, easily seen, for example, in the titles of two collections of poetry, Double Persephone (1961) and Two-Headed Poems (1978);[7] here it suggests the loss of individuality that is the totalitarian regime's goal. (...)

The assaults on the individuality of the protagonists reinforce in both the desperate need to make contact; Winston reaches out to Julia and, fatally, to O'Brien, as the Handmaids (again, significantly, at night) reach out between their cots in the gymnasium to touch hands and exchange names. This need to make contact with others leads Offred's predecessor to carve out the hidden schoolyard-Latin message of hope (Nolite te bastardes carborundorum: don't let the bastards grind you down). The contact itself is a window to a world outside the prison of one's loneliness; Atwood describes it as like making a peephole, a crack in the wall (28–29, 176). The regime works in a variety of ways to sever these ties; "love is not the point," says Handmaid trainer Aunt Lydia (285), aware of the subversion inherent in private relationships. But love is indeed the point for Offred as it was for Winston. It is through Offred's affair with Nick, as through her friendships with other Handmaids, that her re-created self desires and rebels.[10]

Notes

4. Cathy Davidson (24) notes the connection between Serena Joy and Phyllis Schlafly.

5. For love as a subversive force in both novels, see Barbara Ehrenreich, 34–36, especially 34.

6. See, for example, the images of eyes on pages 9, 29, 65, 78, and 84. David Ketterer (209–17) links the eye imagery to that of mirrors in the novel; I myself would be inclined to see the mirror imagery, which renders Offred as only a "distorted shadow," as part of the motif of the double, the danger of losing the self in a world of enforced conformity.

7. Sherrill Grace looks at mirror images, doubles, dualities, and polarities in Atwood's pre-*Handmaid* work.

10. See, on this point and many others, the fine discussion in Constance Rooke, 178.

Works Cited

Grace, Sherrill. *Violent Duality: A Study of Margaret Atwood*. Montreal: Vehicule, 1980.

Huxley, Aldous. *Brave New World*. New York: Harper, 1989.

Ketterer, David. "Margaret Atwood's *The Handmaid's Tale*: A Contextual Dystopia." Science Fiction Studies (July 16, 1989) 2: 209–17.

Rooke, Constance. "Interpreting *The Handmaid's Tale*." *Fear of the Open Heart: Essays on Contemporary Canadian Writing*. Toronto: Coach House, 1989.

Works by Margaret Atwood

Fiction
The Edible Woman, 1969.
Surfacing, 1972.
Lady Oracle, 1976.
Life Before Man, 1979.
Bodily Harm, 1981.
The Handmaid's Tale, 1985.
Cat's Eye, 1988.
The Robber Bride, 1993.
Alias Grace, 1996.
The Blind Assassin, 2000.

Short Fiction
Dancing Girls, 1977.
Murder in the Dark, 1983.
Bluebeard's Egg, 1983.
Wilderness Tips, 1991.
Good Bones, 1992.

Poetry
The Circle Game, 1964.
The Animals in That Country, 1968.
The Journals of Susanna Moodie, 1970.
Procedures for Underground, 1970.
Power Politics, 1971.
You Are Happy, 1974.
Selected Poems, 1976.
Two-Headed Poems, 1978.
True Stories, 1981.
Interlunar, 1984.
Selected Poems II: Poems Selected and New, 1976–1986, 1986.
Selected Poems 1966–1984, 1990.
Margaret Atwood Poems 1965–1975, 1991.

Morning in the Burned House, 1995.
Eating Fire; Selected Poems, 1965–1995, 1998.

Children's
Up In The Tree, 1978.
Anna's Pet, 1980.
For The Birds, 1990.
Princess Prunella and the Purple Peanut, 1995

Nonfiction
Survival: A Thematic Guide to Canadian Literature, 1972.
Days of the Rebels 1815–1840, 1977.
Second Words: Selected Critical Prose, 1982.
*Strange Things: The Malevolent North in Canadian
   Literature*, 1995.
Negotiating With the Dead: A Writer on Writing, 2002.

Annotated Bibliography

Bouson, J. Brooks. "The Misogyny of Patriarchal Culture in *The Handmaid's Tale*." *Brutal Choreographies: Oppositional Strategies and Narrative Design in the Novels of Margaret Atwood*. Amherst: University of Massachusetts, 1993: 135–158.

Providing important, specific information about the Neo-Conservative feminist backlash occurring in the United States at the time Atwood wrote *The Handmaid's Tale*, Bouson explores the crucial intersection of history, storytelling, and interpretation. Arguing that Offred's recurring reflections on her own narration, as well as the jarring surprise of the "Historical Notes" section, work to urge "commentators to reflect on their own critical practices and by suggesting that there are appropriate and inappropriate ways of responding to literary texts." Bouson argues that Atwood, afraid her novel will be dissected and dismissed as an artifact, warns her readers about history's tendency to simply be reduced to lifeless, "safe" storytelling, with the result of making the past less threatening. Thus, Atwood appears to argue for the sanctity of her own work with a postmodern, text-based approach.

Freibert, Lucy M. "Control and Creativity: The Politics of Risk in Margaret Atwood's *The Handmaid's Tale*." *Critical Essays on Margaret Atwood*. Ed. Judith McCombs. Boston: G. K. Hall & Co., 1988: 280–291.

This groundbreaking essay, taking a cue from Offred herself noting that "context is all," explores the novel within the framework of literary, biblical, and feminist traditions. Freibert argues that Atwood deconstructs the West's phallocentrism while also "testing the viability of French feminist theories of women's reconstructive risk-taking and storytelling." Atwood may be a feminist, but she is also a realist, and the intersection between these two world views results in a darkly satiric novel.

Howells, Coral Ann. "Science Fiction in the Feminine: *The Handmaid's Tale*." *Margaret Atwood*, MacMillan Modern Novelists. London: MacMillan Press Ltd., 1996.

Howells, an important figure in Atwood scholarship, discusses in this chapter how the novel acts as a cautionary tale, and how Atwood argues for humanism over strident feminism. Exploring the role of Serena's garden, the role of language, storytelling, and writing, and deconstructing the subtle clues that lie in the "Historical Notes" section, Howells discusses the novel as a work of science fiction, fulfilling the criteria that typify that genre, albeit in a decidedly female-gendered narrative.

Ingersoll, Earl G., ed. *Margaret Atwood: Conversations*. London: Virago Press, 1992.

This collection of Atwood interviews provides students and scholars with crucial information about Atwood's process, opinions, and the ideas that drive her work. The time frame of these interviews ranges from 1972 to 1990, and all of Atwood's work published during this period is discussed, as are more general, but related, issues, such as her thoughts about, and relationship with, the United States, the environment, the craft and practice of writing, and the writer's place in the world, including the inherent responsibilities that come with the job.

Johnson, Brian. "Language, Power, and Responsibility in *The Handmaid's Tale*: Toward a Discourse of Literary Gossip." *Canadian Literature* 148 (Spring 1996): 39–55.

Concentrating on the "Historical Notes" portion of Atwood's novel, Johnson explores the role of gossip as well as the latent values and ideas that led to the evolution of Gilead, noting that the book's concluding section seems to argue that these same notions still lie in the hearts of academics. Because none of the gathered academics appear to notice the inappropriateness of circumscribing a woman's testimony within a title inspired by Chaucer, the *father* of English literature, Johnson claims that patriarchal views are so deeply embedded that they don't register on the radar of even the most educated people. Pieixoto reduces Offred to a manageable fiction, or text, thus demonstrating the danger of Derrida's "comparable exile of the body from language," and making Atwood's novel a cautionary tale against "the ethos of gossip that views the world as a playground and the person as the word."

McCarthy, Mary. "Breeders, Wives and Unwomen." *New York Times Book Review* (Feb. 9, 1986): p.1.

Fellow author McCarthy argues that Atwood's novel lacks imagination; that it does not have satiric bite; and that the characters could have been more convincingly drawn. "I cannot tell Luke, the husband, from Nick, the chauffeur-lover who may be an Eye (government spy) and or belong to the 'Mayday' underground. Nor is the Commander strongly drawn. Again, the Aunts are best." The review is significant because it was one of the few negative responses, and not only was it penned by one of America's most famous contemporary female writers, it appeared in one of the most influential reviews published in the United States.

Rao, Eleanora. *Strategies for Identity: The Fiction of Margaret Atwood.* New York: Peter Lang Publishing, Inc., 1993.

Rao offers an argument about Atwood's treatment of different forms of motherhood: "What the patriarchal oligarchy in Gilead regards as natural, that is woman as 'mother,' is in fact shown to be a cultural construct." Noting the degrees of feminism represented in Atwood's novel by Moira and Offred's mother, Rao discusses separatism among women, and how this "highlights ... the risk of isolation and lack of involvement, whether it occurs on the separatist side or on the liberal feminist side.... These divisions prevent women from achieving a sense of unity, and enable an oppressive regime like Gilead to subjugate them." Atwood's novel thus cautions not only about leanings toward fascism (and censorship), but also about non-involvement. Atwood, Rao argues, urges women not to be complacent at the news of violence against women, but rather to do something and, most importantly, to pay attention.

Rigney, Barbara Hill. "Politics and Prophecy: *Bodily Harm*, *The Handmaid's Tale*, and *True Stories*." From *Margaret Atwood*, Women Writers series. London: MacMillan, 1987: 103–121.

Rigney focuses on the different forms of oppression that appear in Atwood's works, and how these pressures drive Atwood's female characters to, through any means, create or re-create themselves through language. Using multiple works in order to establish a pattern, Rigney demonstrates that in Atwood's world, the price of non-involvement is slavery. In Rigney's words, "no one is blameless, Atwood implies, when it comes to the creation of a Gilead. *The Handmaid's Tale* is a study of guilt and an anatomy of power, but it is also a novel about forgiveness" (119). To conclude, Rigney argues that in spite of the image of writers as isolated from society, the act of writing in Atwood's fiction functions as an "irrevocable commitment to one's society and to one's own humanity" (121).

Rubenstein, Roberta. "Nature and Nurture in Dystopia." From *Margaret Atwood: Visions and Forms*. Carbondale: Southern Illinois University Press, 1988: 101–112.

Taking as a starting point Atwood's seeming fixation with survival and the female experience, Rubenstein argues that in *The Handmaid's Tale*, both are explored in the extreme, expanding specifically on the issue of nature vs. nurture. Regarding nature, Rubenstein mentions the hinted-at ruin of the American landscape, and explores also the persistent, dark use of animal imagery; in more than one way, she notes, Gilead "stinks." To discuss nurture, on the other hand, a term conventionally associated with motherhood and procreation, Rubenstein focuses on hunger, dismemberment, and mutilation, thus turning readers' normal associations on their head. Thus, because Atwood inverts images of both "nature" and "nurture," Rubenstein believes that "the inhospitable environment in which female identity must discover itself" is the inevitable outcome.

Updike, John. "Expeditions to Gilead and Seegard." *The New Yorker* 62 (May 12, 1986): 118–123.

Updike's review primarily focuses on Atwood's Canadian citizenship and how it colors the way the artist views the "colossus" to the south. "Though sharing a continent, an accent of spoken English, and many assumptions with the United States, and afflicted with its own domestic divisions and violence, our friendly neighbor stands above, as it were, much of our moral strenuousness, our noisy determination to combine virtue and power, and our occasional vast miscarriages of missionary intention." Scholars have paid some attention to Atwood's status as a Canadian, placing her within a specific literary tradition, but this article focuses specifically on this particular novel, set in New England.

Wilson, Sharon Rose. "Off the Path to Grandma's House in *The Handmaid's Tale.*" *Margaret Atwood's Fairy Tale Sexual Politics.* Jackson: University Press of Mississippi, 1993: 271–294.

Providing an exploration of how fairy tale archetypes play important thematic roles in nearly all of Atwood's works, Wilson highlights allusions that appear in *The Handmaid's Tale.* She argues that the novel satirizes those who dismiss fairy tales, the Bible, literature, and mythology as mere stories, rather than taking them more seriously, and that "Atwood projects past and present turbulence into the future, structuring a gender nightmare designed to move readers out of Rapunzel towers" (272). Citing the sorts of mythical and biblical figures the key characters resemble, Rose argues that the novel is an anti-fairy tale, one that allows for "the possibility of re-birth: not a return to Eden or matriarchy, but harmony among animal, mineral, and vegetable worlds and peace within the human one."

Contributors

Harold Bloom is Sterling Professor of the Humanities at Yale University and Henry W. and Albert A. Berg Professor of English at the New York University Graduate School. He is the author of over 20 books, including *Shelley's Mythmaking* (1959), *The Visionary Company* (1961), *Blake's Apocalypse* (1963), *Yeats* (1970), *A Map of Misreading* (1975), *Kabbalah and Criticism* (1975), *Agon: Toward a Theory of Revisionism* (1982), *The American Religion* (1992), *The Western Canon* (1994), and *Omens of Millennium: The Gnosis of Angels, Dreams, and Resurrection* (1996). *The Anxiety of Influence* (1973) sets forth Professor Bloom's provocative theory of the literary relationships between the great writers and their predecessors. His most recent books include *Shakespeare: The Invention of the Human* (1998), a 1998 National Book Award finalist, *How to Read and Why* (2000), *Genius: A Mosaic of One Hundred Exemplary Creative Minds* (2002), and *Hamlet: Poem Unlimited* (2003). In 1999, Professor Bloom received the prestigious American Academy of Arts and Letters Gold Medal for Criticism, and in 2002 he received the Catalonia International Prize.

Mervyn Rothstein has been a writer and editor at the *New York Times* for over twenty years, and has interviewed many current authors, including Margaret Atwood, Saul Bellow, Toni Morrison, and Amit Chaudhuri. His articles appear regularly in *Playbill*, *Cigar Aficianado*, and *Wine Spectator*.

Barbara Ehrenreich is a social critic and political essayist who writes frequently on social issues, including gender politics. Her work has appeared in *Harper's*, *The Atlantic Monthly*, and *Ms.*, and her recent books include *Blood Rites: Origins and History of the Passions of War*, and *Nickel and Dimed: On Not Getting By in America*. She has taught journalism at Berkeley and at Brandies University.

Catharine R. Stimpson is the Dean of the Graduate School of Arts and Science at New York University, with a focus on literature and law. She is author of *Class Notes* and *Where the Meanings Are*, along with numerous essays. She has served as President of the Modern Language Association and was founding editor of *Signs: Journal of Women in Culture and Society*.

Amin Malak is Professor of English at Grant McEwan College, Alberta. His writing includes reviews of Salman Rushdie and Ahdef Soueif, and the recent article "Arab-Muslim Feminism and the Narrative of Hybridity." His reviews of Arab and Indian literature have appeared in *Canadian Literature*.

Arnold E. Davidson was Research Professor of Canadian Studies at Duke University. He co-edited *Border Crossings: Thomas King's Cultural Inversions* and *Studies in Canadian Literature: Introductory and Critical Essays* and has contributed or co-authored books on Mordecai Richler, Jean Rhys, and Joseph Conrad.

Marta Caminero-Santangelo is Associate Professor of English at Kansas University. Along with articles on Latina writers including Cristina Garcia, Julia Alvarez, and Helena Maria Viramontes, she is author of *The Madwoman Can't Speak: Or Why Insanity is Not Subversive*.

Glenn Deer is Assistant Professor of English at the University of British Columbia with a focus on globalization and Asian North American writing, and associate editor of *Canadian Literature*. His recent publications include "Writing in the Shadow of the Bomb" and "Asian North America in Transit."

Jamie Dopp is Assistant Professor of English at the University of Victoria, British Columbia. His articles include "Reading as Collaboration in Timothy Findley's *Famous Last Words*" and "The Father in the Mirror: Hall, Harrison and the

Complexities of Male Inheritance." His poetry collections include *The Birdhouse*, *Prospects Unknown*, and *On the Other Hand*.

Pamela Cooper is Associate Professor of English at UNC-Chapel Hill. Her work on Margaret Atwood, Graham Swift, Jeanette Winterson, and Sylvia Plath has appeared in *Modern Fiction Studies*, *Women's Studies*, and *The Journal of Popular Culture*. She is author of *The Fictions of John Fowles: Power, Creativity, Femininity*.

Karen Stein is Professor of English and Women's Studies at the University of Rhode Island. She is author of *Margaret Atwood Revisited*.

Lois Feuer is Professor of English and Coordinator of the Humanities Program at California State University, Dominguez Hills. She is author of "Shaping the Multicultural Curriculum: Biblical Encounters with the Other" and "Joyce the Postmodern: Shakespeare as Character in Ulysses."

Acknowledgments

"No Balm in Gilead for Margaret Atwood" by Mervyn Rothstein. From *The New York Times* (February 17, 1986): C11. © 1986 with The New York Times Company. Reprinted by permission.

"Feminism's Phantoms: *The Handmaid's Tale* by Margaret Atwood" by Barbara Ehrenreich. From *The New Republic* (March 17, 1986): pp. 33–4, 34–5. © 1986 by *The New Republic*. Reprinted by permission.

"Atwood Woman" by Catharine R. Stimpson. From *The Nation* (May 31, 1986): 764–5. © 1986 by *The Nation*. Reprinted by permission.

"*Margaret Atwood's* The Handmaid's Tale *and the Dystopian Tradition*" by Amin Malak. From *Canadian Literature* 112 (Spring 1987): 9–11, 15. © 1996 by The University of British Columbia, Vancouver. Reprinted by permission.

"*Future Tense: Making History in* The Handmaid's Tale" by Arnold E. Davidson. From *Margaret Atwood: Vision and Forms*, edited by Kathryn VanSpanckeren and Jan Garden Castro: 114–115, 120–121. © 1988 by Board of Trustees, Southern Illinois University, reprinted by permission of the publisher.

"Moving Beyond 'The Blank White Spaces': Atwood's Gilead, Postmodernism, and Stategic Resistance" by Marta Caminero-Santangelo. From *Studies in Canadian Literature* 19, no. 1 (1994): 20–42. © 1994 by *Studies in Canadian Literature*. Reprinted by permission.

"*The Handmaid's Tale*: Dystopia and the Paradoxes of Power" by Glenn Deer. From *Margaret Atwood: Modern Critical Views*, edited by Harold Bloom: 93–112. Originally

Index